"UNMISTAKENLY POWERFUL! With every paragraph you will be able to feel the pain to comfort, the guilt to forgiveness and addiction to the path of becoming clean. This read will leave you understanding her sadness turning to guilt and using drugs for answers, while putting her life into perspective after thirty years of questions. Dora's book will make you realize how precious life is and how handling death, alcoholism and forgiveness is the path to overcoming an addiction. You will be amazed at her strength."

- Judith Horn, Photographer

"Grabbing tissues while reading her love letter to Michael, her son, I tried to comprehend how a mother survives the death of their only child. My tears flowed in the gut-wrenching account of his death and funeral. Dora has seen the best and worst of life. She openly shares the experiences as an opioid addict. I could feel her depth of emotions in every line. She is a true survivor. Readers, grab a box of tissues."

- Patty Pascua, LMT, Editor

"*Reflections of an Angel* is a raw, vulnerable, personal account of a woman who has traveled the roads of hell and survived, again and again. Despite being brutalized as a child, abused, the death of her only child, Dora rises above it all time and again. Her journey reminds me that we are all affected by what occurs in our childhood, regardless of whether we think we are or not. I am inspired to rise above past circumstances, to conquer, to keep moving forward. Dora's story is authentic, genuine, real in a way that most are not even close to, moving me to tears more than once. Inspiring, giving hope to all, addict or not. This is a must read."

- Lyn Williams, Intuitive Artist and Designer

Praise for *Reflections of an Angel*

"*Reflections of an Angel* is a powerful story of love and faith, two core components for survival. You become emotionally invested from the beginning to end. This book is a testimony to any grief stricken, chemical dependent addict, and anger issue individual looking for the inspiration for recovery."

- Angela Jones Taul, RN, LMT, Author of *The Mirror of Inner Beauty: Illuminating the Essence of Your Soul*

"I loved how Dora was brutally honest in her words of weakness in grieving and overcoming addiction, it made me want to read more to see her strength in overcoming all she had endured."

- Bonnie Bonadeo, Author, Branding and Speaking coach

Reflections
of an Angel

*A Journey of Loss, Abuse and
Recovery from Opioid Addiction*

Reflections of an Angel - A Journey of Loss, Abuse and Recovery from Opioid Addiction

First published by Powerful Potential and Purpose Publishing 2020

First printing, June 2020

Cover art, graphics and book design by Candy Lyn Thomen - www.CandyLynCreates.com

ISBN: 978-1-7349655-2-0
ISBN: 978-1-7349655-3-7 (eBook)

Published in USA

Powerful
Potential and Purpose
PUBLISHING

www.PPP-Publishing.com
Wilmington, NC

To my angel boy in Heaven,
With every breath I exhale, you are my breath back in.
In Loving Memory of Michael (Spiky) Rains
12.28.71 to 5.20.2020

Thank you, my dearest friend Gloria Coppola, for believing
in me when I didn't believe in myself. Through your
dedication and guidance my dream became a reality.
You are a true Angel in my life.

To all the other Angels in my life,
you know who you are,

Thank You.

Contents

Foreword   ix
Alexa Servodidio

Chapter 1   A Mother's Worst Nightmare   1

Chapter 2   A Drunk Driver Would Change
             Mom Forever   35

Chapter 3   A Father's Love   57

Chapter 4   The Princess Bride   71

Chapter 5   Treatment   87

Chapter 6   My Treasures   105

Chapter 7   A Love Letter to Michael   121

             Conclusion   133

             Epilogue   137

Foreword

Learning to identify your walk in life is essential in finding your peace within the chaos. It may take many years of searching, researching, and discovering to be able to finally recognize your journey. Our walk is our own individual path. A path to establishing, defining, and maintaining a sense of self. Along this journey, there are various positive and negative external/internal factors we will experience. These experiences are stepping-stones which will become our foundations for empowerment. As we find ourselves at the many crossroads of life, take a moment to reflect and embrace your own process.

I was introduced to Dora Sherry when I was honored to have her as a guest on my radio show *Insight Into Healing*. Her story of loss, trauma, and addiction inspired many not to give up, to keep pushing forward and to renew their faith in God.

I firmly believe the work is done in our waiting period. A Waiting Period can be our times of grief, cycles of relapse and recovery, and then our time for healing. Dora has been able to share her story to enlighten others of their own self-worth and strength. Her resilience, love of God and family have become her pillars of strength. I urge you, as the reader, to embrace her story and allow it to lead you to your own pathway of healing.

Alexa Servodidio

LCSW, Psychotherapist, Radio & TV Host, Author

At my lowest,
God is my HOPE.

At my darkest,
God is my LIGHT.

At my weakest,
God is my STRENGTH.

At my saddest,
God is my COMFORTER.

1

A Mother's Worst Nightmare

How does a young mother survive the death of her only child while also battling an opiate addiction? It took me thirty years of hell to finally come to terms with my grief and allow myself to throw away the drugs that held me prisoner. It ruined so much of my life. I am starting this new healing journey to learn how to love myself. This is the story of how my son became my guardian angel, how he has been constantly beside me, watching over and communicating his presence with me for the last thirty years. I believe he has saved my life many times over. My faith in God was tested obviously. Boy was I honestly pissed. I didn't even know it... until now.

I was a high school junior in Kentucky back in the 70's when I found out I was pregnant with my son. Unlike most fifteen-year-old girls who panic when they find out they are expecting, I was thrilled. I couldn't wait to be a mother. A few months earlier, I heard the voice of an angel telling me I would be walking through the gates of motherhood soon. The angel told me God had plans for me. A precious gift was to be born from my womb. He would be special and would change my world one day. Little did I really know what God had planned for me.

Three months past my sweet sixteenth birthday, I gave birth to a beautiful four-and-a-half-pound baby boy. I named him Michael. His lungs weren't fully developed yet, so he wasn't breathing well. You can imagine how frightened I was for my child. I began praying as hard as I could when I heard the angel say, "Don't worry, he is a fighter and he will be alright. Keep your faith in God." Suddenly, my son let out a blood curdling scream and everyone in the delivery room started cheering and crying. I could not have felt happier!

When the doctor laid him on my chest and I felt the warmth of his body upon my heart, I knew God had blessed me. Just then, I saw the angel in the corner blowing me a kiss as she smiled and faded away. My baby wasn't out of danger though. Michael was a full-term baby. However, he was more like a premature baby because of his low weight and undeveloped lungs. They told me I would have to leave him in the hospital to get stronger. Every day for three weeks, several times a day, I pressed my face against the nursery window praying he would survive. He was so teeny-tiny, and my heart was crushed knowing he had to struggle in this lifetime already. My head raced with a thousand thoughts wondering, what if?

The day came when the doctor had a meeting with me. I didn't know what they were going to report. I was a frightened young mama. When they told me it was time to bring him home, I know I was the happiest mom alive. It was the greatest day in my life. I made a vow to devote every moment for the rest of his life to be the best and most loving mother in the world. I only hoped I could live up to it, because he was the most important thing to me. I had hoped one day he would have a sibling, however at the age of twenty, I had to have an emergency hysterectomy. Deeply saddened, it meant I could not have any more children. This made me even more protective and appreciative of this young boy.

As he grew, so did our mother and son bond. He always said I was his best friend and the greatest mom a boy could have. He always made me smile. As time passed, my life was changing and other challenges in relationships would create more stress. I had to admit something when I decided to write this book, something I wasn't proud of. However, the relief and the healing which has taken place, makes me wish I made the decision sooner. I will tell you more about that later. I tend to ramble sometimes and want to make sure you understand how my young man was going to knock me over the head with a compelling question.

Have you ever had a child ask you: "Mom, I know you love God and I'm your only child. What would you do if God asked you to sacrifice me?" Where does a child come up with a question like that I thought. More importantly, why?

As you might imagine, I teared up with a heaviness on my chest as if it were going to explode. This is not something I ever wanted to hear! God already knew what was in my heart, so I had to be honest. I looked at my son and said "I don't know Michael. I do believe my love for God and my faith is strong enough. If He chooses to take you from me for some reason, I will have to find a way to get through the anger. I would like to think I would still love Him and trust Him; however, I would try to honor your life and thank God for giving you to me." Inside, I wasn't sure about any of it. The words seemed to make sense at the time. Little did I know one day I would soon be tested. What was about to happen soon is a mother's worst nightmare.

Michael was so excited when he got his license and his freedom. The day came when he and his friends were going to a party. It was a day I will always remember as the words have repeated in my head for decades. "I love you Mom."

"I love you too, sweetheart. Drive safely and be careful. I'll see you when you get home. Remember to wake me up and let me know you're home." My son was so excited to take his car out for a drive and meet up with some friends for a graduation party.

We had spent the earlier part of the day shopping, even though I was healing from a back injury. It was during this time I had a lot of pain and honestly spent most of my time in bed, drugged up with medication. He so desperately wanted me to go and said "One day, you will wish I were here. So, come shop with me." What's a mother to do?

Pull herself together and get her ass in the car and make the best of his special day and our special moments. He was right, "What IF?"

That evening he was all dressed up, looking mighty fine and a happy teenager, ready to take on the world. He felt like a big man, now that he had his wheels. He had a stride of confidence, a bit cocky too. This big guy was so excited to party that night. I remember him saying "If I died tonight, this is the happiest day of my life, hanging out with you." Good grief boy! Where you do you come up with these thoughts? I was so happy for him and knew he was sincere. However, I never wanted to hear him say, "If I died tonight." This gal had been through enough in life, including watching my mom lose her son. No way was this going to be repeated!!

I have always had angels around me in addition to having visions of things before they occurred. I think it is God's way of preparing me and a gift to save me. When we got home, my son kissed me and told me he loved me as he bolted out the door. I called out to him "I love you, son. You better not be drag racing my car."

"Oh, Mom! Don't worry, I won't. I love you," he said again and that's the last time I saw him alive.

I had no idea how true the vision was going to be when I cautioned him with that 'mother's intuition.'

Michael knew he was past his 2:00 a.m. curfew. So he called at 2:15 a.m. to let me know he was sorry he was late, but that he was safe. He asked me if one of his buddies could spend the night. I told him sure I had no problem. I was pleased he called to let me know. "I love you Mom."

"I love you too baby." I hung up the phone and fell immediately into a deep sleep. Those damned pain meds always knocked me out quickly. I was being cautious, but my back and leg pains were extremely severe from all the earlier walking. I am grateful I heard the phone and my baby's last words. God woke me up, I am sure.

I had no idea my worst nightmare was on the other side of the door when the dreaded moment arrived. My test with God would arrive at the house at 7:30 a.m. Someone was banging on the door. Obviously, I thought it was the boys. Dragging myself, half disheveled, groggy, and certainly not ready for what was about to happen. I opened the door.

There in front of me was a handsome cop, an Italian man, looking very sharp in his pressed police officer uniform. At first, I thought, what had my son gotten into? Some prank at the party? He should have been home by now. What was going on?

Instead, he muttered these horrible words, which I am sure were not easy for him to say. He took a breath, looked at me and sullenly began to say, "Your son died in a car accident ma'am."

I will never ever forget this moment. I nearly passed out when I suddenly thought it couldn't be. It was only moments ago, I was saying goodbye to my baby, never imagining in a million years it would be the last time.

My mind was confused, my heart pounding. I screamed from the top of my lungs and from the depths of my soul, "It can't be. This can't be true. You have the wrong house! You have the wrong mother! It can't be my son! It can't be my baby! He can't be dead!" Louder and louder my words blurted, "You're wrong! You are wrong!" I had gut wrenching screams, as my heart was breaking, and my mind snapping. It all felt surreal. Was I having a nightmare? You know one of those real-life types of dreams. Wake me up someone! That's it, a mother's worse nightmare!

Just then the detective handed me my son's driver's license. There was no denying it. I fell to my knees and screamed "No God! Please not my baby! Please, NO!" I worked so hard to bring this little boy into the world. "How could You take him from me, God?" I cried out. "I thought You loved me. I've loved You my whole life, Lord, from the time my daddy told me You were a good God and the ultimate loving Father. I trusted You, now I'm pissed at You. I love my Michael so much. How will my heart ever heal from this? Why didn't You take me instead?" The why's were swirling in my head over and over and I wondered what did I do wrong? Could I have stopped this in some way? Should I have driven the boys that night and picked them up? All the could haves, should haves, would haunt me over and over.

It has taken me thirty years to admit I was extremely pissed off at God. I was so ashamed of being mad at God because He is a loving God. It didn't feel that way at all now. It wasn't very loving to take my only child from me. That's not a loving God. Seems more like the devil right now! That's right, you heard me! It's like being mad at your dad, even though you love him.

Then, I remembered a few weeks earlier, when my son came home from school and asked me what the story of Abraham and Isaac meant. They were going to perform a play in school with a little comedy twist. He was supposed to be the voice of God. When Abraham raised the axe to sacrifice Isaac, God was to say, "Wait! I was just kidding." My son asked me what made God change His mind in that split second? I told him God needed to know Abraham loved Him more than anyone or anything on earth and the very fact Abraham was willing to sacrifice his son meant he won the test. He got to keep Isaac.

Standing in my living room that day, remembering his question, is probably the only thing that helped me hold it together. This was no comedy, no joke. This was the day I had to start really loving God and trusting Him; not just believing in Him. My anger at God turned into a deeper faith and a deeper trust. He had prepared me with my own child's question. Yes, it was time for me to seriously question my own faith and devotion to God and to start loving myself more too.

"Are you okay?" I heard the police officer ask. Hearing his voice jolted me back into the reality. I was back in my living room. I was sitting on the cold hard floor, rocking back and forth, with my knees in a fetal position, dazing off somewhere. Am I okay? What a ridiculous question to ask someone when their son dies. In a flash, I thought how my whole life was never going to be the same. I don't even know if I had a response for him, because I was so deeply shocked. I was only listening to the voices in my head.

My entire life, I had this inner knowledge. Somehow I knew I wasn't going to get to keep my son as long as most parents do. You could say it was a vision or a voice inside, warning me whenever I would look at him. The voice would say, "Cherish him, because he won't be here long." I would freak out inside when I would think or hear these thoughts. How could I be thinking like that about my son? Why would I hear these words? What could I have done to prevent this nightmare?

A clear and vivid memory hit me. Two years prior, when he was sixteen and just obtained his license, we were driving past the very spot where he would later die. The thought, "I'm going to lose him soon" hit me instantly. Stop saying these things to me in my head! Was I being prepared?

Suddenly, there were tons of people in my house. I don't know how many hours went by. I remember absolutely nothing until they arrived. Friends and family were all loving on me, yet not really knowing what to say. People loved Michael. He was a sweet kid; a big teddy bear and I was always so proud of him. Sure, he was the typical teenager. There were times I wanted to pull my hair when he would get into a bit of trouble. Just like teenagers, he would back talk to me when I took his car keys away as a punishment because he didn't clean his room. He would say, "Mom, that's not fair! Ever since I got my car, you've had me by the balls." To which I replied, "That's why they call them the family jewels and I will hold you by them as long as you live in this house." He would just growl at me and walk to his room.

This little fighter only weighed 4½ pounds when I brought him into this world. I was afraid I might lose this precious angel right from the day he was born. That feeling of loss was so compelling, down to the very depths of my soul. I cannot even start to describe how much it hurt. My whole life was passing in front of me, like a video. I could hear his laughter and I just wanted to be left alone with my memories of him.

People were talking, a lot. Usually like I do. Deep down, I wanted to slap the next person who gave me words of encouragement. I just wanted to be left alone! I started screaming, "Please leave me alone!" I ran as fast as I could to his room, laid on his bed and held one of his stuffed animals. If you've ever lost someone, you probably know we can smell them. You try to feel them one more time and feel close. I would do anything to find a way to connect to Michael. I locked the door and cried my heart out. I feared I would be haunted for the rest of my life and never sleep well again. How could I ever sleep again when I couldn't believe this myself? What had I done to somehow have made this happen? I genuinely thought I would be the first person to die of grief. Obviously, God had a greater purpose to keep me here to share this story.

Oh God, I hear the kids now, all of Michael's friends. Go away! I can't face you all now. They were always around in my house, hanging out with Michael. I loved having the kids at the house. Now, they're in the other room crying and screaming. I must get up and go out there. I have to find some way to be strong for them. This is how I became so stoic in my life and strong. I had to be like a soldier, a general even. The one being the re-assuring one, making sure everyone else was okay. It's quite interesting how we find the strength to console others, while we are the ones dealing with deep loss and pain. Perhaps it was a saving grace, because, inside, all I wanted to do was be the one who died, not him.

At that point, I would have taken poison if it would have numbed my ripped-out heart. How was I going to bury my precious baby boy? Pop a few pills. Were there enough to numb me out? Xanax, an anti-anxiety medication, was a blessing to me and would become a good, best friend. It immediately started to numb my mind and nerves. I spent the night hugging and consoling one after another of my son's friends and assuring them everything would be alright. All I could see on their darling faces was how hurt and scared they were. They needed someone to be strong for them. That was me. I was always the strong one, and I stayed true to my nature.

The most unreal day of my life came. How am I going to do this? It was time to go to the funeral home. I must pick out clothes for my only son to be buried in. I still felt like this was all surreal, still questioning how this happened. All I could do was cry nonstop, and pop more pills, while my family helped me get through this process.

My mom lost my older brother to a drunk driver when I was a little girl. History was repeating itself. How can this happen again in our lives? What meaning is behind it, if any?

By now the police had shared exactly what happened that night. Michael's friend was in the car with him and witnessed everything. Fortunately, this boy survived to share the details of what happened, including how a man was staggering down the road. I would learn much more in the coming days.

I didn't know what I was going to see at the funeral home. I found out Michael saw the man's body fly in two directions upon impact. When he overcompensated, turning the steering wheel too hard, he hit a curb and flipped the car over onto the sunroof. I remember saying to him one day, "If you ever flip this thing with the sunroof open, you will die." That is exactly what happened. The car flipped over the curb and he died of suffocation. My baby was unconscious and could not breathe. I felt a relief with this knowledge. Michael would not have been able to live with himself knowing someone died because of him.

Even if it was or wasn't his fault, we never know God's reasons. On some level, God protected him from this nightmare. My angel baby would not have to feel his own physical pain, dying instantly, nor the pain of someone else dying.

The dreaded evening arrived, and my body could not move. I felt like my feet weighed a thousand pounds. If I go, it will be real, and I wasn't ready to face this truth. Nor would I ever. Instead, I sat in the car for approximately 45 minutes. It felt like hours and yet, it felt like seconds. All I could think was, I can't do this! Over two hundred of my son's friends would be there, including my family and friends, holding me up as I walked, bent over, slowly up the aisle, to the casket, to view my baby for the first time.

When I finally opened my eyes and looked at the body lying there, it wasn't him. Oh my God. It's not my baby! His face had been damaged so horribly in the accident; it didn't look like him. I was so sure it was all a dream or just a huge mistake. Once I cleared the tears from my eyes, I could see his hair. That's his hair. Oh my God, those are his eyebrows!

I knew his lip was cut because I kept rubbing my own lip for two days. My lip was raw and almost bleeding. I kept rubbing it, saying something's wrong with his lip. I reached out to touch his lip. I heard people say, "Don't let her touch him. Dear God, don't let her touch his face."

Thank goodness the funeral director said, "Let her touch him, that's her baby." I touched his lip and I touched mine and that's the last thing I remember before passing out. This was much more than I could handle. It was the truth. He really was dead.

I woke up in one of those dreary dark rooms in the funeral home with someone brushing my hair and someone else trying to give me a Xanax. I remember telling them I cannot tranquilize this way. They insisted I take the pill. However, deep inside of me, I was afraid my own addiction would resurface if I did. They said the doctor prescribed it. Yeah, my doctors always did, little did they know how easily. I must get through this. I had all these kids here who needed me. What's a pill or two, right?

I got myself together and walked up to the casket. I was numb and I didn't know where I was or what I was feeling. It's like watching a movie. You see hundreds of people marching by, wanting to give you a hug, hoping they can find the right words to console. I would look into their eyes, see the pain on their face and it would magnify. There are no 'right' words. There were moments, though, I wished they would all disappear so I could just go home.

The children broke my heart, they were so hurt. None of them knew how to handle it, how could they? They were all looking to 'mommy' Dora to tell them what to do. I hugged each one and I promised them it would be okay. I assured them I was all right and would continue to the next child and repeat the same thing. Was God giving me this strength to help others in this moment? How could a grieving mother handle these gut-wrenching moments when she wasn't okay? I just wanted to die. In the back of the room I noticed a familiar face. My Daddy. "Oh Daddy!" I cried when I heard his voice. "This hurts so bad," I said while he wrapped his arms around me.

"I know baby, I know," he said. He did know, because he lost his child, my brother, when he was only ten years old. He would, and did, understand the depth of this horrid and empty feeling for sure. I remember how strong he was, a man of God. When I was younger, my brother had been hit by a drunk driver while riding his bike. Now the same nightmare was playing out again. Except this time it was his grandson. It all came back so clearly, even how my dad held the driver in his arms, forgiving and consoling him while it was his turn to bury a child.

Today, I realize as I write this, how many years I had stuffed my own grief way down to help console others. Perhaps it is because I saw Daddy be so strong, always helping others. I thought this is what was expected of me too. I had no idea how many emotions would surface writing this to help someone else.

During this time of grieving I would crash again. I would hide and cry all night long, not even answering my phone or doorbell. My friends did not know what was happening and probably thought I was drunk. The healing process began. Finally, I know my addiction to pain meds numbed me out. I am trusting God to help me through this process.

The funeral is a blur. I was so shocked, numb and heavily drugged, I cannot remember most of what happened. I barely know how I got to the gravesite. I do recall some of the words my brother-in-law said at the eulogy. I don't remember most of it because I was still in shock. Everyone mentioned he did a wonderful job. Huh? A wonderful job and my baby is gone? That doesn't even equate in my head. What's so wonderful about all of this?

I hardly remember sitting at the graveside, staring at the casket. The voices were far away as I stared into nothing, not hearing anything they were saying. I had so many thoughts flying inside of my head. So much pain screaming inside of me. Tears flowing, my mascara dripping down my face. I didn't even care! This can't be happening, I kept telling myself. I remember someone trying to hand me a rose or flower from the casket as we started to leave the cemetery. I abruptly slapped it away and I said, "I'm sorry. I guess I'm a little angry."

A little angry? That's an understatement! I was pissed!

On the evening of the funeral, after everyone was gone, it was a great relief to have some quiet time. It felt peaceful. I know they all meant well and we needed each other, all his friends, laughing and telling stories. The memories were good ones. I guess that's what we do, remember the good times.

As I opened the door to let one last friend say his goodbye, I saw the most beautiful sight. Something that would make me feel closer to my son than I have ever felt in life. It was his first sign. It would let me know he is my angel and still here.

One perfect flower. I had waited six years for just one flower on this little peony bush. My son had even taken a picture of it a few days before his accident, just in case something happened to it and it didn't bloom. It had about 50 buds on it and only the one in the middle started to grow. It was a little light pink petal, starting to peek out. We were all so excited we were finally going to get one flower.

The day it was planted, I remember saying, "Dear God, I just need one flower." I had faith I would have a world-famous flower one day. If I just had faith. Just give me one flower, dear God, to show the world. There it was, in all its glory, blooming for Michael. Michael's friend said, "No, it's blooming for you. That's Michael saying, 'There's your one flower Mom.'" My prayers were answered. God is there for us in the right timing.

I went back in the house and sat to read the pages of all the beautiful notes his friends gifted me. It was such a precious feeling to know how much they loved him, how he taught them to be family. In that moment, I was a proud mama. It was time for me to rest and I hoped I could.

At 1:30 in the morning I was wide awake and remembered the flower. There was a driving force compelling me to go outside. I sat in the driveway holding this precious flower to my face and just cried into it. I can still smell the fragrance of it thirty years later and feel the dew drops on my cheeks, my chin, and lips. I whispered into the flower and said, "I love you too baby and I'm going to miss you." It was amazing how close I felt to him at that moment. "Thank you for being my Angel on earth and thank you for being my Angel in heaven."

Three days later I heard the news reporting my son had killed a man. It infuriated me. My son was not a murderer! I felt horrible. This was injustice, a lie and it was torturous! I was pissed. I would come to find out from a friend that there was some conversation happening at the local bar. The same bar where the man who died had been drinking that unfortunate night. This friend overheard people saying, "He needed a ride, someone should have given it to him." That didn't make me feel better, needless to say.

I felt compelled to confront the person at the bar because I was mad! I ordered a shot of tequila from the bartender and asked her, "What is your name? Are you the girlfriend of the man who got killed last week?" She nodded. "Well let me introduce myself, sweetheart. I am the mother of that boy being accused of murder. You and I need to talk and get a few things cleared up." Lovingly as I could, I expressed that someone should have given this man a ride if he was drunk. She agreed with me. No one murdered anyone, I expressed. "Things happened when he stepped out onto the road and we will never know why. I would love for you to let this mother grieve in peace." We cried together and then prayed. We learned we had similar upbringings and both our dads were ministers. It was really a loving and forgiving time for both of us. I drove home thinking, "I got that done, resolution and peace in my heart with her."

I believe that my dad laid that first core value in my consciousness, when I saw him forgive the man who killed my brother.

Sometimes bad things happen to good people. We must trust God. He knows why and that's all we need to know. Today, I'm glad I had that little boy for eighteen years, some never have this blessing.

I choose to thank God for that and not be mad anymore. I choose to deal with my grief now and start healing. I choose to put a forty-year opiate addiction away and not be sick and tired anymore. Yes, opiates took over my life in so many ways. I pray God provides the strength and all the people I need for support to keep me on the straight and narrow. I must do this now!

Writing this story and going back to that scary place, the place I was so afraid to go to for thirty years, has given me so much healing. It has taken so much of the deep hole away from my heart. I don't need pills anymore. I need to start living my life now and start trusting my Angels when they talk to me. I must stop ignoring them like I've been doing all these years. They've been screaming at me from everywhere, while I kept covering my head and ignoring them. I was lying to myself and others. Now, I'm going to rise and fly with the angels. I'm going to make the best of my life from here on out. I have great people holding me accountable. I have a better vision of my future, supportive friends, and help, including my angel baby who all remind me that God is here for me every day.

The only consolation I have now is I know Michael's here with me. He is my Guardian Angel and shows himself all the time. I'm always writing stories about how 44 appears in my life. That was his favorite number. When he was a little baby and reaching for building blocks, barely able to sit up, he would reach for two fours. When I asked him one time why he loved that number so much, he just said, "I don't know Mom. I just always have. There's something about that number that feels special to me."

I feel Michael was the one who 'accidentally' threw my pain pills in the washing machine a few months ago when I was thinking about writing a book. Honestly, how could I be truthful in my writing if I wasn't being honest with myself? I took this as a sign. That morning, I had my pills laid out on my bed, counting them, when the doorbell rang. I quickly covered up the pills with my sheet. I didn't want anyone to see them nor did I want my cat to eat them.

I never would let myself grieve for fear of dying of a broken heart. Eight years after my son died, my marriage ended in an abusive situation that almost killed me. I spent the next twenty-two years making bad decisions and taking as many pain pills as I could get my hands on. Oh, I had a few times in those years I would quit the opiates and then something emotional in my life or something physical would happen to charm me back to be with my old friend, opiates.

Don't be afraid to grieve like I did. The fear will destroy you. It's relieving beyond imagination. I wish I had known this in my life. Keep crying, tears are healing. That's why God gives them to us, not to just anoint our eyes but to clear our hearts. My father once said, "If you didn't have grief, you wouldn't have love." "Concentrate on the memories," he would say. Dad was a minister who said, "If tears were only there to lubricate your eyeballs and keep them moving, they wouldn't need to fall down your face. Tears fall because that's the wash cycle. It really does all come out in the wash."

Thirty years later, after my son's death, I'm realizing I didn't get to grieve or forgive myself. I'm still grieving my son. I love to tell the funny stories about him because he was such a comedian and such a cute kid. I realized this was my way of stuffing the grief so far inside and drowning it with pills. It is only now it becomes clear how far down the rabbit hole I went all these years. I wasn't even realizing all the signs Michael was sending with his favorite number 44. This has been a wake-up call for me. He was showing me God didn't give up on me. All these years, there were signs to have faith and hope. Michael was saving me when I couldn't save myself.

Whenever I was most distressed and taking too many pills, the 44 shows up. I always feel like a huge bear hug is touching me and even as I am writing this, tears are flowing with my sniffles. It's such a miracle for him to always communicate with me this way. It really gets my attention.

You see it happens all the time. One day I went to the store and was looking for a jar of spaghetti sauce. At that very moment, a man reached up and said, "Try this brand." Was I seeing correctly? On the inside of his wrist was a tattoo with the number 44! I asked him "What is the symbol of your tattoo?"

"It's in honor of my son, only eighteen years old, who passed away in a car accident on May 20, 1990." How can that be a mere coincidence? That was the exact age and date my son died! I just stood there crying because I knew my son was there again, helping me get through another rough and challenging detox.

Michael and I loved to collect pennies. It was the anniversary of his death and another day

I would down those pain pills. It was always such a struggle remembering that day. Later, when I could pull myself out of the bed, I decided to go to the cemetery and talk to him about my addiction to oxycontin. It felt like he was really listening. Once I was done, I headed to the store for a quick stop. As I was coming out, I saw something shining on the ground. Since I love sparkly things, I bent over to pull it out of the asphalt and guess what? It was a penny! Not just any penny from heaven. It was the one Michael still needed for his collection. Okay kid, you are getting really good at this, I thought. It was a 1944 penny! His collection was now complete.

Now if I could just stop these pills, life would be different. I decided to take a ride to my friends' cabin on the lake. There on his wall was a license plate displaying the numbers 4444. Seriously? Again! I know I'm stubborn and need lots of reminders. Should I laugh, cry or be amazed? What are the odds my precious angel would send me two signs? "What is this?" I said to my friend.

He replied, "It was the first license plate I ever had." I just stood there thinking, Michael is here again. Each time it always felt like the softest touch from heaven, the sweetest kisses in the world on my cheek.

The next day, I realized I did not even remember being at the lake house. This was getting ridiculous! I had to check myself into a treatment center for my opioid addiction, once and for all. As my tears began to flow again, I was scared. I was thanking my son for not letting me die again.

When my friend, who just happened to be a book publisher, told me a few months ago she wanted me to write a short story for a book with other collaborative authors, about my son's death, I panicked. The last thing I wanted to do was go back through it all. It was too hard the first time and why relive it now? I was afraid of that time in my life. I started writing and the tears poured with grief as the words appeared and something magical happened. By the time my story was finished, I was feeling a thousand pounds lighter and it was the most healing experience I could ever have had. I never realized how therapeutic writing could be for our transformation.

Years later I would return to Ohio. It was a sudden decision and I felt guided to go back. No one really understood why, and neither did I. I was living in beautiful sunny Florida and now I'm freezing my butt off here. My sister gave me a jacket and I pulled on a cap over my head and off I went.

The first place I went was to visit Michael's grave. My car automatically drove to the exact spot. I felt compelled to be home.

I was driving through the cemetery when a rush ran through me. I felt whole and complete. I didn't feel lonely or alone again. I felt like I was home. It was almost hard to write this as I am choking up reminiscing and sharing all of this. Sniffling and dribbling, the tears cleansed my heart and soul. When I saw the head stone, I smiled because it has his picture on it. Even though he didn't have a smile in the picture, I was happy to see his beautiful face. I didn't feel like I needed to say anything because he is always with me. I'm quite amazed how wonderful I feel and not tempted to drink or take pills being here with him again. Don't get me wrong. I have challenges but I'm faring well, and I will be okay.

Writing this, Michael has given me passion for my life, a goal and a purpose. It's giving me confidence in myself again and I haven't thought of pain pills now for months. Even my energy is coming back. I love you baby boy, thank you for watching over me. Thank you, God, for giving us your son and for giving me mine and thank you for taking them both back with you. I can almost understand how God felt. All that grief was released, and my angel is finally able to guide his mom on a new and wonderful journey to healing.

I realize my son, Michael, has been watching over me all these years. Now I made the decision, finally, to deal with my opioid addiction. I am so grateful for every angelic sign he sent to me these past decades and I thank God I'm alive to share this story with you. Look for the angelic signs in your life, they are always there.

I am enjoying my life again and I am excited to share this book about my life with you. I am letting my angels guide me now and praying that I can help someone else who might be struggling. I can help other parents in life get through the loss of their precious babies. God is going to align me with a church where I can share my story with those who need to hear my words, receive my support and strength, and know we can and will survive.

There is nothing to be afraid of more than ignoring it and letting it eat you up inside. Facing my greatest fear is what finally freed me of the pain. It has given me a passion and a purpose again in my life. I'm working on taking a long hard look at the things in my past that caused me to seek out those pills. If I can come to understand myself, I can make better choices for my life now. I can really enjoy the rest of my years in peace and happiness with a knowledge of my authentic self and living life to the fullest. I can release my son from the pain I was holding and let him fly in happiness knowing his best friend is going to do great things now and is finding happiness inside instead of pain.

For now, I am home. I am peaceful.

"Of the Angels he says,
'He makes his Angels winds,
and his ministers
a flame of fire.'"

Hebrews 1:7

2

A Drunk Driver Would Change Mom Forever

You would have thought Mom would change her habits when my brother got killed by a drunk driver.

You could always find my beautiful mom at a bar on weekends. That was exactly where she was, partying the night she got the news of her son's death.

My brother was minding his own business. Carefree and happy as usual, on a beautiful day, riding his bike on a Kentucky country road. I was only seven and looked up to him. He was my best friend.

I laid in bed that night and looked over to where he slept. It hit me he was gone. I felt so alone, so scared, a mere little girl. I was seven years old with bright eyes and blond hair and loved my best friend, my brother. I was going to spend many nights crying, trembling and afraid because Mom was nowhere to be found. I needed her to hold and comfort me. She just couldn't. She was so angry when she heard the news and most likely in shock as I was when my son died. As a child, I could not comprehend her behavior and why she would want to drink more. It simply added more fuel to her state of mind and she wasn't available for any of us or herself. Now, looking back, I know how I learned to numb myself out.

Mom would be blind to the nightmares that were going to come into my life due to her neglect.

My older sister would move out eventually as she was tired of all the neglect and abuse. My baby sister, well, let's say I became her caretaker when she was a 2-year-old toddler. Quite the load for a 7-year-old little girl. I remember my brother and I laughing a lot. He loved to entertain everyone with his silly jokes and stories. How would I get along without my buddy?

I remember blaming the drunk driver. I believed at the time he was the cause. It was his fault I would be raised by an alcoholic mom. The truth is, I was listening to my mom blame him. She had the same drinking issue long before this happened. She even blamed my father for my brother's death. She was fueling the anger stored from their divorce. It eventually turned to hatred and rage inside of her, making her sick as she aged. There were so many deep emotions within that woman, I could hardly understand it all growing up. Even today, I am still trying to make sense of it all.

I can still see her, the night she was holding my brother's blood-stained clothes, crying and begging God to bring him back. Even though I needed her too, she didn't seem to notice the innocent, broken-hearted little girl at her knees or the other children. I was desperately trying to get a morsel of comfort, receiving nothing to ease my own pain. My feelings didn't matter anymore. I would grow up observing Mom's lifestyle, how she manipulated men and how the booze took control of her every time she got a paycheck.

Mom had many health issues along the years. I would watch her lean into the porcelain toilet bowl time after time, and I would be busy cleaning up her vomit and blood. Everything around me was falling apart. No matter how hard I tried to fix things, including her, it only made me sadder. I wanted my mom back but that was not going to happen.

Mom ruined her first marriage to a caring man, my dad who was a Baptist minister, and then would repeat it again. She remarried another caring man years later but she didn't appreciate him. One night when I was eleven, I decided to run away. I didn't even think about the dangers that might be lurking in the night. I just wanted to get away from the screaming and fighting between the two of them. My head and heart could not handle any more of the constant stress. I prayed for an answer as I wandered the streets aimlessly by myself. Step by step it got darker and colder. I had no idea where I was going or what I was going to do.

I recall thinking now, how a mother is supposed to be there for her child's needs and pain first, instead of her own. Her first choice was always booze. It was her baby bottle. No matter how much my mother loved us and would work to stay sober for months, there would always come a time when the pain would overcome her. Alcohol would destroy our lives again. I imagine her pain was guilt related.

Now as a young pre-teen, I had no idea one day I would feel that way too.

The walk was long, and I had no idea how much time went by. I was sad, scared, alone and tired. Suddenly two men were following me and asked me what I was doing all alone on these streets. Naively, I chatted with them and told them my story. "I have no place to go," I said. They seemed kind enough and offered me a safe place with them for the night. I got in their car, not realizing they had also been drinking. Dear God! I just left two drunks and now I was in a car with two more! How could this be? I had no idea I was going to be unable to escape a horrible fate in the next moment.

We rode around in the country, listening to music for about an hour or so. It was kind of fun. They kept popping open beer bottles, laughing, singing, and having a good time. Something in the air shifted in a moment. They began to drive towards an area I knew was not good. They turned around looking at me and telling me I was so pretty. I became frightened. This wasn't fun now. I wanted to get out of the car. We were in a field, somewhere deserted, when the car stopped. I was terrified as they started petting me, screaming at them to STOP! I pulled away. They told me to be quiet and it would be over quickly. I bit them! Next thing I saw was a fist coming at me and I was knocked out. I woke up briefly while they were sexually molesting me, taking turns. It was dreadful and I feared for my life. Each time I tried to fight them off they would hurt me even more. When they were 'finished with me', they threw me from the moving vehicle. I landed in a field where a farmer would find my small and frail body the next morning. I was beaten beyond recognition and wearing only one sock. My clothes were gone. I was naked. The farmer had noticed his crop was flattened out, went to see why, when he found me nearly dead. I can't imagine what would have happened to me if this angel hadn't come along to rescue me that morning.

It was ten days later when I woke up in a dark, cold hospital room all by myself. I was confused and didn't know how I would get home. The nurse brought in some men as I pulled my body back and hid under the covers. They were detectives, asking me what seemed like a million questions. My child like mind was spinning. I was still hurting terribly, and I was terrified. What if they found out who did it, what would happen? What if they went to my house and found my mother in a drunken stupor with beer cans everywhere? They would surely take me away from her. I was trembling inside, trying to figure out what to do. I didn't want to make another bad decision. So, for all they knew, I was Jane Doe and I wasn't going to say anything more. I kept lying and I was getting good at it by now. I felt deeply embarrassed, violated and ashamed my virginity had been taken away. I didn't know who or what they would believe. What if I told them and those two men found me and killed me?

I was so nervous to go home. I was sure everything was my fault and Mom would blame me for getting in the car with those men. I had so much shame dwelling inside of me. I was feeling broken and dirty. I honestly didn't know what to do. Was I really a bad girl? They continued to ask me questions about my mother. Dear God, hadn't I been through enough? I was not going to tell them anything else. The authorities said I left them with no choice. They placed me in a nearby children's home, where I would spend the next seven weeks, alone and no one missing me.

The next several weeks would not be easy as it felt more like an institution than a home. It was certainly not where I wanted to live anymore. My mother never even reported me missing. I did not understand, how could that be? In the meantime, life was miserable. There was a bully teasing me daily, even though I defended myself. The day came where I began sobbing so bad, I could hardly breathe and broke down. I poured everything out to my counselor. They immediately sent a case worker to see my mother to inform her what happened. She immediately accused them of lying and directed the caseworker to get her another beer from the kitchen refrigerator. I can't even imagine what the caseworker was thinking in that moment, surely quite shocked. I can't even fathom why my mother didn't report me missing. Didn't she love me anymore? She had already lost a son. Could she handle losing a daughter too? Was she so self-absorbed and oblivious to time, she had no idea how many weeks had gone by? I will never know.

The next morning, they informed me I was to have a meeting with the director of the children's home along with my mother and father. The fear was so strong, I began to panic, and my body went numb. I felt intimidated. The thought of facing my parents, in the same room, was scarier to me than anything that might be waiting for me behind the office door. "Dear God," I prayed, "please don't let her be drunk."

Of course, my beautiful mom would show up all pretty and sober. She would dazzle the men, I'm sure. She had make-up on, her long brown hair was curled, draping very sultry around her face and shoulders, as if she were going out for the night. I wondered what people would think because she looked like a good mom at this moment. The director began to question her, as she hung her head in shame. "Did you know what happened to your daughter?" Her response was dreadful. She could not remember a thing, she said, when the counselor went to her home that day. In that moment, I felt like an orphan and unloved. How could she forget me and not care about me? I won't ever understand that and even now I feel a deeply hidden anger emerge. I didn't even realize that, too, was numbed out for years. My drug dependency was doing the same thing Mom's always did. Hide the feelings, bury them and they will all go away.

All I wanted to do was run into the arms of my father when I saw him. I knew he would rescue me once again. However, I was terrified of my mother. I could not betray her. Surely, I would be punished. I just stood there. I was listening and praying God would make everything better. A decision had been made while I watched my mother glaring with hatred at my father. She looked evil. My dad gained custody of me. While it made me feel safe, I saw the intensity in my mother's look and could almost hear her say, "Everything is your fault, Dora." The silence in the room was deafening. I felt like it lasted forever. I did not know what to say, feel or think. I felt my mom was right. I did something wrong. I questioned myself "Did I ask to be raped?" I know I could not stop those men from hurting me that night. Just as I could never stop my mother from hurting me and herself night after night, in her drunken state. I was so concerned about my little sister, only six years old. What would she do, who would take care of her while I was gone?

At the same time, I felt a great sense of relief and happy to be with my dad and stepmom again. It was always peaceful living with them. They were happy and kind, and dad was always so loving and compassionate. I needed my dad more than ever now because my trust in men was broken, totally gone. Dad was a good man, a minister. I could never understand why Mom didn't treat him with the respect he deserved. He showed me not all men were bad, and I could always trust him for everything. Dad would never hurt me. I believe my level of compassion towards others was a beautiful by-product of what my dad taught me.

My mother was my greatest cheerleader, and always told me how beautiful I was. She would tell me with my looks and personality, I could get anything I liked from men, if I played my cards right. It reminds me today of that song, *Fancy*. "Just be good to the men and they will be good to you." That was not always the case growing up, however. I would encounter many abusive relationships, not fully understanding how I would get myself in hot water again.

I missed and loved my mom at the same time. I had no trust in her promises. She always said she wouldn't drink another beer, only to find her popping beer cans and ignoring the kids. I was scared of what might happen to me the next time. As an adult now, reviewing my life, I see why I numbed out so much of my pain, along with the how and why many addictions began to unfold in the coming years. They say children learn by what they observe. I am grateful to have observed two sides of life with my biological parents. One gave me the faith and hope to carry on, while the other was teaching me how to get everything I wanted.

Perhaps both helped me survive.

I would spend the next several years observing how Mom used men like a box of tissues. Pull one out, use it and throw it away. Another was already popping up and waiting to be used. So, it was natural for me to follow suit, right? Yep. I discovered I loved feeling pretty around the boys when I was fourteen. They would tell me they would do anything just to be with me. I came to discover, at this young age, my own power of sexuality I had over men. It wasn't the power, I would later learn, that would get me what I really wanted in life. They had something I wanted, and I had something they needed. "Yes, Dora," the words would ring in my head, "Be nice to the men." I had no idea how many times it was going to backfire in my life, causing me more grief, pain, and heart ache. I remember Mom telling me, "Do you have to be like an outhouse fly?" This meant she didn't approve of my dating poor boys, even if they were kind and I liked them. She'd rather I found a wealthy one instead of landing on shit.

That was my mom. She didn't even know how funny she was. She was a straight-shooting wise woman with a lot of street smarts. I seem to have inherited a lot of that from my mother, including her comical sarcasm.

Mom was so happy about the birth of her grandchild, Michael. She loved him more than anything in the world and he adored her. He always said he had his grandma wrapped around his little finger and she thought he was perfect. That's exactly how she felt about him too. With all the stuff I went through in those dark times, I knew it wasn't my mother's fault. It was the alcohol. I can see now after stopping my opiate addiction, how much of a hold addiction had on her, and how it became more important than anyone or anything to her. I know because many times that was my own life. Selfish in many ways, it was the only way I understood how to numb the emotional and physical pain I would experience in life. I'm glad today I had that understanding of her, because it certainly made it easier to forgive her.

I realize through my own healing; a child of an addict is scarred for life. Forgiveness would be the key for myself, as well. The addiction can lurk in the dark, waiting for you, holding you a captive prisoner even if you swear you won't do it again. Taking responsibility and being accountable is a huge step for me. I swore so many times I would never be addicted to alcohol like my mother. I would end up doing the same selfish act, making excuses, lying, and trying to numb my pain. I never associated the pain pills with my mother's addiction until now. Different drug but the same way of dealing with it. Oh yes, I drank too. I didn't acknowledge it until one day my counselor said, "Dora, you traded one addiction for another."

The sins of the mother do repeat themselves sometimes. Children grow up to repeat what they see in life, not what they're told. Maybe watching my mother, I learned it was the way to handle my grief without even realizing it. I thought I was doing OK, even though I knew I was addicted to pain pills. I wasn't an alcoholic. I wasn't anything like my mother or so I thought. I'm learning more about myself, my patterns while writing this story. I am so much more like my mother in so many ways than I imagined. Over the years, many of her bad decisions and addictions became my foundation of understanding and entered my life and become my own addictions. Including the same addiction to men she had. I didn't even realize it until a few months before putting this all down on paper. So many events in my life have paralleled my mother's in very eerie ways.

When I was fifty-three, I watched my strong-willed mother lay in a hospital bed fighting for her life from a ruptured aneurysm in her brain. The doctors implied it was from years of drinking and just coming off another long binge. The doctors didn't expect her to live. However, with Mom's strong spirit, she rallied. They had to operate, cutting diagonally through her brain which left her unable to speak or communicate with us. We weren't sure if she knew who we were or if she even knew who she was for a long time.

After months of rehab, Mom learned to speak and walk again. She had amazing resilience. I learned from her too. Over the next couple of years, she gained enough independence to live on her own in a cute little cottage house. My sister and I would visit her all the time and enjoy Mom's wonderful meals along with some laughter and joking. It was the mom I always imagined and wanted. We loved to gang up and pick on her over all the funny things she used to do and say. She would laugh and tell us she didn't know how we ever managed to still love her after all she had put us through She never drank again after that aneurysm. We are so thankful to have had her final ten years sober and happy to be alive.

Mom was humbled and her heart seemed to open. Every summer she would take grocery bags, fill them with vegetables of different kinds and take them to her neighbors as gifts. It was one of her favorite things to do. Mom worked as a nurse's aide most of her life and absolutely loved the job. She would come home and tell us all the funny stories about some of the patients. We would giggle about it while we were cooking dinner together. It was a joy and blessing to enjoy her in those last years. It was the greatest gift my mother gave us. I am the strong woman I am today because of her and I wouldn't have any other mother in the world.

In the last few years of her life, Mom developed lung cancer from years of smoking and her health started to decline rapidly. During one of her stays in the hospital, a young minister came to visit her. She told me how much she liked him when she got home from the hospital. There was something about him she trusted for some reason. I couldn't believe that my mother was saying something good about a minister. I called his office and told him of Mom's wish to see him again. He rushed over to her house and spent several hours sitting with her. He read the Bible to her, answering every question she had about it.

I had never seen my mother talk about God or the Bible. It was an experience which brings tears to my eyes now. I heard her ask him if he thought God had punished her by taking her son, because she had broken her promise to serve Him forever. I'll never forget how he smiled at her so tenderly and said, "Now, Wilma, does that sound like the God you know? It doesn't sound like the God I know. God is a loving Father, not a punishing one. May I ask you," he said, "When did you start believing you have as much power as God?" At that moment, I could feel my mother's heart healing and releasing all the pain. She was finally at peace in her mind and heart. She finally found the love she craved for her whole life in God. Everything Mom and I went through in life, all the struggles, the arguments, and fights about her drinking, disappeared as I watched my mother smile while he sat there, holding her hand, and praying with her.

Mom was always of the belief you couldn't get into heaven unless you were baptized. Before the minister left, she asked him if he would baptize her before she died. "It would be my honor," he said to her.

Mom never got well enough to go to church. On the last day of her life, when she was in the hospital and dying, my younger sister, Sheila, called the minister. She asked him to come to the hospital to baptize her. "I don't know if she will know you are here," she said to him, "at least Mom's dying wish will be granted." Mom had been mostly unconscious for two days with no response. When he walked up to her bed, put his hand on hers and told her he was here to baptize her, I saw my mother smile.

I went to church with my dad many times when I lived with him, listened to him preach and watched him baptize people. I was always touched by it. Until now I had never felt anything like this. That day was auspicious, watching this handsome, young minister baptize my mother. Knowing she knew what was going on, made it such an incredible miracle to all of us. She found the strength and responded with a smile to each of his questions. He sprinkled her with holy water and said a prayer with her to meet God in peace.

A few hours later, I stood there with my Sisters, while my older sister sang hymns to my mother. My younger sister asked me if I had a cross. She wanted Mom to have a religious symbol in her hand when she died. Two days before, I had been gifted a beautiful gold cross I was wearing at the time. I handed it to my sister. She placed it in Mom's hand, then placed her head on Mom's chest. She could feel Mom's breath moving in her body and hear the heartbeat one more time. It was a beautiful moment.

Mom died peacefully and quietly in that moment. We had the chance to talk to her about the pain we experienced through her years of drinking before she died and were able to heal a lot of wounds. The scars will remain forever. It seems ironic to me now, the same year my mother stopped her alcohol addiction my opiate addiction got worse.

In the end, it didn't matter how many times Mom tried to apologize for the things she did. The damage to my life was already done. I grew up not loving myself enough. I'm sixty-four this year, the same age my mother was when she died. I'm coming out of addiction like Mom did. I pray I can follow her example of trying my best to make amends and apologize to the people I've damaged. I will forgive myself for the things I did and the things I was not aware of.

As I was sitting writing this story, after moving to Ohio to live with my sister, I looked down. I realized the coffee table I was writing on was the one Mom bought over 50 years ago. I didn't realize my sister still had it. We laughed together about how many times Mom got drunk and tripped over that coffee table, never spilling a drop of her beer. Thank you, God, for another gift from my mother. Thank you to my Angels who guided me to come back to the place I grew up to finish this book and begin my new life. My healing journey took me back home to the little girl with the pale blonde hair with big green eyes and all those huge dreams she had for her life. I'm finally at peace with God, like Mom was with the minister. Now I know why she was smiling.

I dedicate this chapter to my mother, for giving me the courage and strength to throw away my addictions today. Mom, you were a wonderful example to me in so many ways. I love you and I'll always miss you until we meet again in heaven.

"Keep on loving one another,
as brothers and sisters.
Do not forget
to show hospitality to strangers,
for by so doing
some people have shown
hospitality to Angels
without knowing it."

Hebrews 13:1-2

3

A Father's Love

My knees were shaking and my heart pounding against the lump forming in my throat. I finally found the courage to tell my father, the Baptist minister, the news I had been hiding from him for months.

I believe Dad was a gift from God. I was the last born of his three children, his precious little baby girl. How was I going to tell him this terrible secret I was keeping? He was always bragging about how perfect I was to the people at church. What would he say now when he discovers his fifteen-year-old precious daughter was carrying a child?

I had never felt anything but love and acceptance from my father and I knew he was going to be hurt, I never anticipated the look of disappointment he was wearing on his face, let alone the intense anger that flew at me.

"What were you thinking laying down with that boy!" he shouted. "How exactly do you think you are going to raise this baby?" I was not prepared for this reaction. The man who always showed compassion to others, even to the man who killed his own son, now had none for me.

I was not taking it seriously according to my dad. He called my grandmother and asked if I could live with her until the baby was born and put it up for adoption. My father's solution to the problem.

I knew only God could give me a baby. If I were not supposed to have it, He would not have planted the seed in my womb. Did not my father always say God's plan was perfect? He never made one of us without a reason. I was not about to give God's greatest gift to me away to anyone.

"I never want to see your face again!" were the last words he said to me as I walked out the door. I was shocked, guilty, and devastated! How could he be so angry and throw me away? I was so happy, why would he be so angry? I wanted this baby and I was in love!

When my son was born, I understood what my dad meant by me being a gift from God. That is exactly how I felt about my son. I wanted to call my dad to let him know he was a grandfather, but I remained silent until five months later.

I was not going to give him a chance to refuse to see me. I kept it secret I was coming and with determination I would show him God's gift, a grandson. My stepmother would enjoy him and love him, I knew. One way or another, I decided to work this out. I was not going to give him a second chance to turn me away. My heart was pounding so hard I could hear it, my knees so weak I could hardly stand, as I waited for the door to open.

I didn't know if my dad was still going to be mad at me. I knew I could not live any longer with bad feelings the way they were between us. I stood my ground. I waited with my sweet baby boy in my arms for whatever reaction he might have.

His look was soft, full of love and prideful again when he saw me holding my little baby boy. My father put his arms around me, and suddenly everything was alright. Later in the evening, I had a chance to apologize for letting him down. He smiled and told me he was sorry he had disappointed me by not being understanding and supportive. He sat quietly and watched as I took care of my son's needs, rocking him gently to sleep, snuggled in my arms. I could feel how proud he was of his little girl.

The same father who was mad at me for being pregnant was now telling me what a good mother I had become. He said I was right to fight to keep my child. Dad shared his feelings and saying he felt he had not shown me God's love and understanding at the time. He was proud of me for the faith I had in God at a time when he questioned his.

We laughed about the time when I was eight years old and kept interrupting his sermons at church with my talking. He decided he would teach me a lesson by embarrassing me and making me get up and give the sermon the next week. If I wanted the attention all the time, he was going to let me have it. He was going to sit back and enjoy while watching me squirm with embarrassment.

It was during this time I was learning some hard lessons in life about honesty. I decided then to do my sermon on the topic of honesty. I was going to teach him a lesson now and the brat in me began to plan my sermon. I stood in front of the pulpit on Sunday, with a chuckle under my breath and told everyone that my dad was teaching me about being honest. I didn't know if he was going to kill me as I began preaching about honesty. "He wasn't being honest himself, though you know, because I had to keep his secret. He sneaks and smokes cigarettes on the drive home from church every week." Dad rushed up to get me off there as quickly as possible. No words can tell you how fast my father interrupted my sermon that day. On the way home from church, while telling me how proud he was of my honesty and willingness to express it to everyone, my father threw his cigarettes out the car window. He thanked me for the lesson he got from my sermon. I was actually proud of him and myself.

There was another time when my mischievous self continued to interrupt his sermon, Dad closed his Bible and announced to the congregation, "Dora will be giving the sermon next week." Keeping his word, I was in the pulpit the following Sunday. Being new to bible stories, the only thing I knew was a few of the ten commandments. I proceeded to tell all the church members what that meant to me personally. "In my house, the first rule is you don't wake Dad up in the middle of the night. He gets what we call 'the Big Eye' and he can't go back to sleep again. Rule number two is you don't scream SHIT in church no matter how many mice run by." Yes, Dad would learn to be mindful of putting me up there to preach.

Dad had a good sense of humor and he told me he had been trying to get people to jump out of their seats for years with his preaching. I had accomplished getting him out of his seat faster than he ever thought possible on my first time. My father was convinced I was going to be a wonderful preacher just like him one day. I laughed when Dad told me this because he could never figure out if I was sent from God to be a test or a testimony.

When I asked him why God makes bad things happen to good people, he told me if I tripped and fell while he and I were walking, it was not because he made me do it. It was to make me look where I was going the next time. It was not his job as my father to stop me from being hurt. It was my father's job to hold me until my wounds healed, like God does through the bad times.

Our relationship grew even stronger over the years. He adored his grandson.

The night he came after Michael died; I threw myself into his chest. The tears streamed down my face from my broken heart. I was begging Daddy to make this nightmare go away. We stood together by the casket, my head on his chest and his arm around me. We said goodbye to our precious gift from God. We had come a long way from that little girl who was afraid to tell her dad she was pregnant. No one understood the love I had for my child like Dad and God. God sacrificed His only son for us, and he felt the pain of losing his child too.

My father reminded me while standing there of the story how God holds us through our pain. "If God did not allow grief, love could not exist. The grief you are feeling right now is so strong because of your love for your child. It's a gift some don't experience. You must remember our children are gifts from God. How we treat them is our gift back to Him. You raised such an Angel. God must have wanted him for His own enjoyment," he said to me.

Dad shared his abundant wisdom and guided me through this great tragedy in my life. "We must appreciate what He gave, without us deserving it. I want you to remember while you are working through your anger at Him, to thank Him for giving you this gift in the first place. Remember how angry you were at me when I tried to take him away from you at birth? You forgave me, and your love kept us together so I could be here for you today." He always knew exactly what to say to make me feel better and bring me closer in my relationship with God.

The effects of Dad's Parkinson's disease were beginning to show themselves in the withered arm he had from his childhood struggle with polio. His one good arm was no longer of much use to him either, at times. He would freeze up in the middle of moving, like a statue. We would have to stop and wait until he was able to function again. There were times he forgot who he was and who we were. The progression of the disease made it difficult for my stepmother to take care of him by herself. I wanted to spend as much time as I could with my dad. Over the next five years, I became comfortable in my car, driving five hours each way. He would call saying he was having a hard time and needed his baby girl to help him. My father needed me, and I was going to make sure I was there for him whenever possible. I told my dad one night I had driven two sets of tires off my car. We chuckled.

The hospital hallway seemed different this time somehow. There was a soft light outside my father's room as though guiding me to him. For a minute, I was sure it was an Angel. I stopped at the door this time instead of immediately rushing in to hug my dad. I was captivated by what I saw and felt compelled to be still.

My stepmother was standing beside my father's hospital bed when I entered, wiping the sweat from his brow with a cool damp cloth. I heard her saying to him, "I know it is not the same as when your baby does it. It will have to do until she gets here." She didn't realize I was listening at the doorway. I saw and felt the strength of their love for each other. I felt the love they both had for me. I watched her taking care of Dad right to the end of his life. When I took the cloth from her hand and started wiping his brow, I saw him struggling through the paralysis. It was now affecting his facial muscles as he tried to give me that charismatic smile that charmed me.

As sick as he was, Dad never lost his sense of humor. One of his favorite pastimes was picking on me and trying to make me laugh. As he looked at me in that precious moment, I was cherishing every moment with him. He blurted out, "What took you so long? Did you have to stop and replace those tires a third time?" I fell in love with my dad all over again as he made me chuckle. I smiled at him and responded with, "No Dad, this time I replaced the whole car. I bought a sports car so I can get here faster." I spent my time praying with him and singing his favorite songs to him as always. He would laugh so hard when I would imitate him preaching and remind him of all the practical jokes he used to play on me. He would beg me to stop because it was going to kill him before anything else did, from laughing so much.

I was always trying to surprise Dad with some crazy funny thing I had done. He would try to surprise me back with something more fun and surprising he had done.

While sitting with my stepmother making the arrangements for dad's funeral, I noticed a large picture of my father when he was ordained, hanging on the wall in the office at the funeral home. My dad preached at many funerals there and was well known by everyone. He was such an example of courage and strength. Because Dad had a true unconditional love for God, the funeral home wanted to show honor and respect for him.

When I thanked the director for putting it there for us that day, he told me it had been hanging on the wall for several years. It would hang there forever as long as the building existed, and funerals held. My dad earned so much respect in his life ministry. It was amazing to discover this man hung Dad's picture in his office, long before he knew he was going to bury him. The rebellious little girl who told her daddy's secrets in church was now sitting there wishing she had listened to more of his sermons. I knew right then I wanted to be like Dad. The little girl who thought he was crazy when he said I was going to be such a great preacher, began to dream of doing exactly that one day.

The greatest gift God ever gave me is, and was, my father . The greatest gift my father ever gave me was to teach me about God. Dad's strength gave me mine, no doubt. When I saw my father putting his arms around the drunk driver who killed my brother, forgiving him in that moment, he laid the foundation of my faith in God. For this I will always be grateful. He showed and demonstrated to me how God loves us.

So how would I end up getting caught once again in another addiction cycle? My relationship with my dad was everything I dreamed of. Yet the pain and heartache of losing my father fueled my opiate addiction. Once again, the monster showed up in my life.

I am grateful for the lessons of compassion my father taught me. I believe it was this core foundation which helped me forgive the many people I would encounter in life who would hurt me.

May you be showered with Angel
Blessings today!

May the Angels bring you peace,
happiness, hope, and Divine comfort.

May you be healed of whatever causes
you pain.

May your whole life be filled with
Divine Love and Angelic Light.

©2020 Candy Lyn Thomen / Candy Lyn Creates

4

The Princess Bride

I always wanted to wear a jeweled crown and be the princess of a manor. My dream was about to come true. I was the beautiful Lady with golden hair, walking on the picturesque estate where I was living. It's a divine 200-acre deer farm. This particular day I awoke with the excitement of a child on Christmas morning. It was my wedding day! Imagine how I felt to have turned my life around.

I was the elegant Lady of the Manor, sipping my morning coffee with my prince charming, my fiancé. The kitchen was a favorite spot of ours. We would look out the bay window, while colorful peacocks danced before our eyes. Have you ever seen the vivid, golden shine upon their royal blue and green feathers? We could see the wedding coordinator and decorators making the preparations to ensure everything would be perfect. I was happier than ever on this bright, shiny early morning.

You know the song from *The Sound of Music*, when Julie Andrews sings, "I must've done something right." That's how I felt in this moment. I was thinking what a beautiful life God had given me. It felt like a Disney movie, all magical and glitzy!

No more would I run home crying or be called white trash.

I began to think, "How did a child of an alcoholic single mom from the wrong side of the tracks grow up to marry one of the most successful businessmen in town? God, are you going to do something to punish me? Will you eventually take this away? Please God, this is too good to be true." I couldn't trust it even though I wanted to. Today, I am a princess and it feels pretty damned good.

I am afraid honestly but happy.

I went to feed the baby deer after drinking my coffee and prayed my fiancé would not turn into a monster or villain. I've seen enough of those, especially coming out of a very abusive marriage a few years previously. I easily recoil and go inward, every time someone raises their voice. The shrill terrifies me. I never want to hear it again.

God, you gave me a jackpot after feeling hopeless, scared, out of money and sleeping on my sister's couch. I was hungry and exhausted mentally. I needed some time to get my head together. I needed someone to come along and rescue me. Thank you so much for hearing my prayers.

Okay, no more time to reflect. I had to get ready for my wedding. I was going to have a lovely day of pampering, getting my hair all pretty and nails done. Everything would be perfect. All I could think of was getting to the church to marry the man of my dreams. I tend to be a little late for things and wanted to be sure I was on time today. I didn't want to upset my fiancé either. My bridal party looked like beautiful princesses. Wow, I better take a deep breath. This is really happening!

The minister was standing outside the church chatting with the florist. He was making sure everything was perfect for us. He greeted me and took me aside. Jokingly, he told me I had just a few more hours to change my mind. I looked at him and of course my sense of humor came out. I loved to embarrass my pastor just a little bit sometimes. I was known to be a comedian with a touch of sarcasm. I looked at him and said, "No, I can't change my mind now. I already told the baby deer earlier this morning we were getting married and they won't be illegitimate anymore." He laughed, like he always did, with that little blush of pink across his cheeks. We walked hand in hand to the room where I would prepare for this amazing union. He made me feel calm.

I looked at the floor and saw the gown delicately draped around my feet. I felt like I was in the middle of a fairy tale. Even though I had been married previously, this was more perfect than anything I ever wore. It was a gorgeous platinum-colored princess wedding gown.

Standing in the chapel doorway, I watched the bridesmaids lead the way. My knees were shaking as it was my turn to greet the man God wanted me to walk along side with in life. Dressed in his tuxedo, I could see him shifting back and forth on his feet, waiting for his woman to join him in marriage.

Doubt entered my head at that moment. Am I really the woman of his dreams? Was he really my

Prince Charming? I loved him because he was gentle, kind and had a generous heart. I knew he was going to give me the life I always wanted. I wasn't always the best judge of character in the past, and I wanted this one to work.

What am I thinking? The man is perfect for me. So what if he yelled at me the other day when he was stressed. Get over it, I thought. There will be times you will yell at each other. That's what a marriage is about, right?

"Stop it Dora!" Trust God and His angels this time. Don't ruin and sabotage another relationship based on your past. Go down that aisle now! Marry the man you love.

I proceeded towards the altar, holding my pastel-colored bouquet. Inside the bouquet was a black jellybean, tucked way down. Michael always gave me some for my birthday. After he died, I saved the last one he gave me. I was so sure Michael sent my fiancé to me; it was a good luck charm. I tied the silver ring Michael loved with a ribbon around my garter. I took Michael with me. My heart pounded and I was excited for our future.

The ceremony was so special. A single extra

candle of unity representing my son was burning. We both knew he had blessed this marriage and was smiling in heaven. We lit the two unity candles for Michael and lit the one together to represent our union. The princess bride was kissed. Happily we strolled down the aisle to greet our guests.

Flowers adorned the entrance of our property. Everything was elegant. The entire property had been transformed into a fantasy land. I felt I was on the set of the show, *Dallas*.

The reception was perfect. Seven hundred plus people celebrated with us. I never felt happier in my life or more sure of anything or so I thought. I had it all. I had the perfect man. I was surrounded by friends.

Everyone cried when we had our first dance together. They were so touched by our love for each other, as we gazed into each other's eyes. Handsome and strong, he swung me around the dance floor like a fairy princess. My head was spinning too, you can imagine. A little girl from rags to riches was about to enter a new journey.

At the close of our first night of marriage, we had one more thing planned together. Our favorite little vehicle, the ATV we frequently rode around the farm, was a little secret adventure for us. I didn't know my husband had hidden a bottle of champagne earlier with two beautiful elegant His and Her goblets. We wanted a quiet moment together to start our life where the gentle deer roam.

This simple little ride would soon change everything. Neither one of us had planned for what was about to happen. We were just so happy to begin our life together. The wind picked up as we happily toured around the property, talking about our honeymoon. Suddenly, the dress caught around the tire, jerking me abruptly off the vehicle and pinned me to the ground. My neck was injured. I am lucky I didn't break it. I know for certain an angel saved me that night.

The next morning, I woke up in a lot of pain. We were supposed to be leaving for the French Riviera in a few days for our honeymoon. I didn't want to cancel this amazing time together. This can't happen! I called the doctor immediately and went to have him evaluate the injury. It wasn't as bad as I had imagined, mostly a soft tissue injury. Thank goodness. He began writing on one of those little pads and handed me a prescription for pain medication. I hesitated for a moment, for fear that my opiate addiction would return. I was desperate though and didn't want to ruin our honeymoon. I didn't need them for emotional pain, I thought. How bad could it be if I take them for my physical pain? I will just take them this one time. "Did I really need them," I questioned myself? Somehow, I felt I messed everything up and destroyed things again. Why did I ride the Gator ATV in my wedding gown? I realize now, this trauma brought up emotions from my past. I was frightened.

Obviously, the honeymoon wasn't the romantic trip we had hoped for. My heart was about to be broken again. An impatient man, I had come to know, yelled at me the first night of our cruise. I can hardly remember why now. All I thought in my head was, "How can you scream at me?" I thought I was doing everything perfectly, even pretended I wasn't in pain. I was upset, didn't feel worthy or understand what I had done wrong. Maybe the pills erased my memory of what had really happened.

My perfect life had been shattered by anger. My perfect dream was collapsing right in front of my face and I felt responsible. I had to do something to fix it. It wasn't long after returning back home, I was back at the doctors to refill the prescription. I wasn't physically hurting this time. I was dying emotionally, and scared. So many memories from growing up haunted me every time he yelled when he was stressed or became impatient.

For the next nine years, I was high many times. I know I did things to hurt my husband, because, on the inside, I was mad at him and perhaps myself. I couldn't tell him how I felt. I thought I was being ungrateful. Less fortunate people were happy, and I wasn't with all he was providing me.

How could I be so self-centered and selfish? All I thought about was myself. I allowed a tiny, little pill to destroy us both. I didn't know how to handle my emotions. No one taught me. I didn't know how to speak about them. I went into hiding with my friend, Opioid.

My perfect marriage became one of fighting, arguing, and screaming at each other. Just like my mom! I couldn't believe it. Once again, I had messed up and ruined everything. Today, I believe if I had help when I was younger, I would not have been so touchy about his outbursts. I don't think it was as bad as I thought.

Over the years, I was treated like Julia Roberts' character in *Pretty Woman*. I got to do things I never imagined when I was a little girl. I remember prancing into a boutique to pick out a few evening gowns for events we had to attend. I walked in there wearing what I would call commoners clothing. Five hours later I felt like a queen. The best part was, as the owner of the shop rang up my beautiful outfits, she began to cry. Her granddaughter needed surgery and the commission on the sale would give her enough for the down payment. I felt very happy for her and grateful my purchase could help someone in need.

I strutted out of the shop with my fancy custom bags and beautiful gowns, feeling on top of the world. I was going to wear an elegant black gown at an upcoming country club event. This would be my first! I had also purchased a gold one, one of those fancy mermaid style dresses. That was going to be sexy for sure. Surely, I was going to make his eyes spin in his head when we walked arm in arm together at the next fund-raising event.

Imagine my surprise when I flew for the first time on his personal jet! Talk about feeling famous! I could pinch myself. Was this real? I was looking quite sassy, country girl beautiful with my pixie haircut, tight jeans, and sweatshirt. We were flying to our home in Florida for a quick luxurious vacation. The life I was living was magical. It even included housekeepers and cooks! Why was I so unhappy?

My frustration stemmed from being emotionally damaged. I had zero tolerance for loud voices. Without realizing it, I had started self-sabotaging everything when he would vent, even when it wasn't aimed at me directly. Don't get me wrong, I loved my life and him. However, I was emotionally unavailable.

It was during this time I became a full-blown synthetic heroin addict. I put my husband through hell rescuing me. Rushing me to hospitals and doctors to get my fix. Until one fateful day he said I had to choose, him or the drugs. "I can't live this way anymore! Which one do you love more?" he asked.

I used the excuse of numbing my emotions and now a choice had to be made. I finally stopped taking pain pills. However, it was too late for the marriage. The damage had been done. I was already feeling like a drug addict, constantly messing up and causing problems. During the nine years of our marriage he was extremely frustrated with me.

Being very disappointed with myself, I ended it. I regret leaving the marriage because I loved that man so much. The more pills I downed, the angrier he became, and the more scared I got. The ugly cycle continued. I can't, and don't, blame him. I would be angry too if I were him.

I'm learning how to take care of and love myself. This is not an easy task as I tend to be very hard on myself. I see looking back, it wasn't his anger that ruined the marriage. It was the scars from my childhood, along with my deep insecurities which caused me to sabotage it before it could fall apart.

I can't help think, as I sit here now, I may have had the happily ever after life, had I not reached for those pills on that unfortunate day. I could say "if only" a thousand times. The reality is like the beauty and the beast, I had to see how much more value there was with inner kindness, over the superficial qualities. Appearances had much more value with my upbringing. Mom had coached me to live by a *Fancy* character which obviously didn't work.

How can you be good to someone else, when you don't know how to be kind to yourself? I have since told him how sorry I was, and am, for everything I have put him and his family through. Although I never hear back from him, he is always in my prayers.

I made some decisions that things would and will be different. My goal would be on family and community. I would accept responsibility for all my actions. How could I fail?

"Help me, please!" I cried out once again to my angel Michael, in heaven. He never let me down. "I need your magical angel power now." What did I do so wrong? I don't believe God would punish me. All I wanted was a kind and gentle man who would love me for myself. Would I ever find true happiness? Did I even deserve it? One day I would finally realize I had to love MYSELF.

No matter how long
you've traveled in
the wrong direction,
you can always
turn around.

- unknown

Treatment

"Hello, my name is Oxycontin and my problem is Dora."

Yep you know it, I was the issue. I invested more money into my addiction than I ever considered investing into myself. When I think back of all I could have done to help this world, boy did I waste a lot on drugs. Those who have addictions, even if it is chocolate, cigarettes, or coffee, think about how much money goes into it monthly. You would be amazed how it adds up.

You know I messed up my marriage. So, let me tell you what really broke it apart. My regrets run deep.

Oh, how I loved waking up at our summer lake house. The sounds of the boats on the lake going off for a relaxing day. The men out early, fishing, to see who could catch the biggest fish. Neighbors walking around with their little dogs for a delightful morning stroll.

This morning would be different when I woke up. I didn't have a clue how I got there. What was I doing in this bed? It was wintertime. Why was I at our summer house, which was an hour away from our home? My head hurt and I needed my drugs. I struggled down the stairway to the garage, where my car was parked perfectly, hoping to find my purse. My husband was nowhere to be found and neither was the purse. I was definitely more than a bit confused. I needed to clear my head. Try to think, Dora, what happened the night before? You don't just wind up somewhere, without a reason, right?

I went to my beautiful bathroom upstairs. There it was, right where I guess I left it the night before. Those precious gems in my purse. Everything seemed perfect, yet still no memory of getting here. I reached in my purse and grabbed those precious 80-milligram oxycontin pills. I ground up two of them on the fancy countertop in the bathroom to snort up my nose. I caught the horrible image of myself in the mirror. Who was that person? What had I done? In a few moments, I knew I would feel normal again and put this all together. I hoped.

Everyone envied me. People assumed I had the greatest life in the world. I was loved by many. When I walked into a room, I could turn heads. My beauty was intoxicating at times. Yet, here I was, in my beautiful summer home, snorting drugs up my nose. Not a pretty picture. I didn't know who that gray-looking woman was looking back at me. She looked old, worn out and tired. I didn't recognize myself. What did they envy? I was miserable, distraught, and hiding behind everything, not to be really seen.

Ah, a little Saline solution up the nose to get the oxy into my system faster, and downstairs to the kitchen for a cup of coffee. I had to figure this out. Yes, this was my daily routine. Oxycontin and coffee. The breakfast of this addict. That's how I started each day. This day, I knew I was in big trouble.

I called my friend and asked her to come and get me. I knew I had gone too far. I asked her to help me get treatment. I confessed I had a terrible drug addiction and I had been hiding it from everyone.

I guess I hadn't been hiding it as well as I thought. She already knew where I was. My husband had called her in the middle of the night and told her I had left after a terrible argument. I had no memory of it, whatsoever. Can you imagine how that felt? I've never been so scared or humiliated or embarrassed in my life.

She was so kind and said she would be on her way to help me. As I continued drinking my coffee, all I could think of was my mother and how she used to binge drink. It was embarrassing to all of us. I was doing the same thing to my husband. He was probably annoyed at something or at me. He may have raised his voice. So off I went, fleeing for my freedom, running to hide somewhere safe and quiet. Now, I am learning, through the counseling I'm currently receiving, I have a pattern. I get desperate and run if I fear something or someone. I prefer peace and quiet, unable to tolerate arrogant, upsetting, screaming voices. I was about to learn a lot more about myself, things I never imagined.

It was comforting to know all I had to do was ask for help. I found myself, later in the evening, waiting to board a plane which would take me to Florida for an in-house 30-day drug treatment program.

My friend and my husband arranged it all for me.
I packed my clothes, and as I left, all he said to me
was, "I love you, please get better." I knew no matter
how much he loved me, this wasn't fair to him. I felt
tremendous guilt, unworthy and broken. I hurt him
so badly, not really knowing or understanding why
I would do that. Here he was hugging me goodbye.
I didn't want to hurt him anymore or hurt myself
either. I just wanted help at this point. You know
relationships have challenges and we don't always
get along. We have difficulties and sometimes
experience emotional confusion. I had to figure out
how to fix this.

I remember, twice, while I waited to board the
plane, I slipped away to the bathroom stall to snort
the precious, burning, stinging, magical stuff into
my nose. I was afraid and hopeful all at the same
time. However, I had to numb my feelings. It was
what I had grown accustomed to doing. On the
plane I must have gone to the bathroom five or
six times. I'm sure I had at least thirty or forty,
80-milligram oxycontin pills in me that night. What
was I thinking? That could kill a horse!

It was nearly midnight when an older gentleman
met me at the airport. He introduced himself and
informed me he was driving me to the treatment

center. He could have been anybody for all I knew, or cared. I barely remember being on the plane. I don't even remember the ride to the treatment center. When I got there, it certainly was not the posh or a fancy place I thought it was going to be. Treatment was not going to be a vacation. The Lady of the Manor wasn't in her comfort zone by any means. She wasn't very elegant at that moment either.

This isn't for me! What am I doing here? I don't belong here!! I desperately wanted to turn around. I knew I was ruining everything. I was torturing my caring, loving husband and myself. It had to stop.

It was lonely and scary in the dingy little hospital-like room. It was the Infirmary at the treatment center. I was listening to some of the other patients puking their guts up, screaming from their painful detox and all I could do was sit there, feel sorry for myself and cry. A nurse came in and told me they were going to search me. That really scared me. I wasn't quite sure just what she meant by that. I was extremely relieved to find out she was talking about searching my purse, my clothing and nothing else.

I got about four hours sleep that night, still in my

clothing. I had collapsed on the small bed. The next morning, they took my blood pressure. They made me drink some orange juice with something called methadone in it to help me with the detox. It was one of the worst things I ever had in my life. I had such a horrible reaction to the methadone. I was dizzy and high. I couldn't stay awake. I was already detoxing from my oxycontin. I was doing better, before they gave me that horrible, nasty, stuff. It was a God awful feeling.

I never felt high on the pills. Methadone knocked me down to the point I couldn't stay awake. It took everything I had to keep my eyes open for the meetings. I felt like shit, it was horrible. They insisted I had to take the methadone even though I told them it made me feel worse than the actual detox and I didn't want it.

My first day in treatment was not looking all that great to me. I was scheming in my head how to get out of there. I went to get a cigarette out of my purse. Out of habit, I looked in the zipper part and I couldn't believe my eyes. They hadn't done an adequate search. I asked the nurse if she would like the 131 oxycontin pills I still had. Imagine her surprise! The night nurse had totally missed them.

I can't tell you how many times, in the next thirty days I wanted to kick myself in the ASS for giving them up. I guess I really did want help after all. I was proud of myself for being honest. Frankly, it took a lot to hand the pills over.

I was supposed to spend the first three days in the medical department for detox, before I was put into a dormitory-style house with the other ladies. For some reason, the very next morning, one of the girls came from the treatment house to get me. She showed me where my room would be and how everything worked. I couldn't even hold my eyes open, let alone talk. No one seemed to care. I was having such a horrible reaction to the methadone and nobody would listen to me. I kept crying, telling them, "Please, I'm overdosed. I've been drugged." They just laughed at me, telling me when I came in I was already drugged, that I was going through their program now and if I didn't take the methadone, I would suffer worse.

That horrible feeling came back, and I felt like trash once again. I felt different from everyone else. I wasn't one of "them." I would not say, "I am an addict or alcoholic," at the meetings. That's bullshit, I am not. This was so humiliating!

I got up the next morning and went to the Medical Center. When I refused to take the methadone, all hell broke loose. They accused me of being rebellious and not wanting to follow the rules. They threatened to throw me out. In my mind, I thought go ahead. I threatened to take the $28,000 certified check back which I had in my purse for them. I will happily walk out the front door.

"Throw me out," I said. They called my husband, while I packed my suitcase. He told the nurse, "Listen, I know her well enough. Let her try without it. If she says she can, she can." My back was killing me, my entire body aching, a horrid headache and still I felt better than taking that other crap which made me high.

I didn't feel like I belonged there. I wasn't a drug addict. I was using my drug for physical pain, not to get high. In our group meetings, many shared how they could not stand being sober. They wanted to be drunk and numbed out. I never wanted that intoxicated feeling. I just wanted pain relief.

I went through treatment and I hated it! For the first three days, if I wasn't sleeping, I was crying nonstop. It was nothing but writing letters to my mom and dad, both who had passed away. Who gave a rats ass? Give me somebody who can help me stay off drugs, instead of trying to psychoanalyze me! I never actually voiced it to anyone. I followed all the rules, did everything they told me to do. Including all the goofy, crafty things. I felt like I was in a nursing home, even sitting through the silly games they played.

I did meet some amazing women. I heard some incredible stories I can't repeat but will never forget. I found out I was not alone being an addict. There were other outstanding, classy women, celebrities too. We all had something in common. We all had pain inside, trying to drown it with drugs or alcohol.

I was shocked at the first lecture. I walked in and saw what was written on the board. One side said Heroin/Oxycontin. The other side had all other addictions. Oh, FUCK! I am a heroin addict! I had no idea oxycontin was synthetic heroin, until I read that. It scared the hell out of me. I sat there, just staring at those word, repeating them over and over again. I was going to have to face something bigger than I could have imagined. This began my wake up call.

A few days later, I finally had some free time to escape to a little gazebo in the garden area by myself, to complete an assignment. I was going to have to really face my addiction and the real damage it had done, the toughest challenge I would have to admit. I had to add up how much money I thought I had spent on drugs. I'm embarrassed right now to even say I spent $150,000, maybe $200,000. That's when I broke down and sobbed like a baby.

"Hello, my name is Oxycontin and Dora is my problem," I said one day at a meeting. Everyone laughed, but it was true. When I think of all the good, I could have done to help children in the world with that money, only to stuff it up my nose. I knew right then and there, I was the problem. I had lied to my husband, every one of my friends and associates. Who knows who else? I hid the drug addiction as hard as I could, for as long as I could. I couldn't hide it from myself anymore. Honestly, I didn't even feel guilty enough to change my ways.

I was told to write a letter apologizing to my husband, confessing to him everything I had done. I loved him so much. He was so supportive and never once made me feel bad about spending money. Yet somehow, after the first time he yelled at me, when I saw anger coming from him, I pulled away. He could never really reach me again. I had shut down emotionally, for good.

I could barely get through the days and nights at the treatment center. I would cry all night, not sleeping for two or three nights at a time. Then I would have to do all the sessions, classes, lectures and the Alcoholics Anonymous meetings. It was tough but I did it.

There was about twenty-five women altogether at the center. Every night, when someone would finish their thirty days, we would all sit in a circle celebrating them. We shared what we learned from them, giving them greetings, and rounds of cheers, wishing them the best in the world. It would be a wonderful celebration. I was very proud when I graduated and felt all their love.

As soon as I got home from treatment, I went back on Vicodin and eventually Percocet. I thought they were okay, not realizing they were also a problem. I needed something for my back pain and had taken them before and felt like they weren't as bad as oxycontin. I needed something and thought this was a safer choice so I was comfortable with them and knew I would never take another oxycontin again.

Little did I know at the time, they were equally poisonous and sucked me right back into the addiction. Remember, once an addict always an addict!

Over the near few years I suffered with headaches and more drugs were prescribed and poured into me.

I'm in a little bit of shock right now, thinking of the many days, weeks, months, years of my life I've wasted, either being drugged out, not remembering what I did, or sleeping in bed for days at a time. It was nothing, for me, to go through 150 to 200, 10-milligram Vicodin a week! I can't even believe I'm alive with all the drugs I've taken. I have more angels protecting me than one can imagine. How could I take them for granted?

That magic pill got me every time. It controlled my whole life for forty years. I hope and pray I can spend the rest of my life showing others there is always hope.

I'm certainly not proud of the things I did and I do forgive myself. I will be writing letters to those I love, begging their forgiveness for the pain I caused them. I guess this chapter will be my letter to the ones I love, to the ones I cannot reach. To all those angel people God has brought into my life who have supported me, despite myself. I love you all. I'm going to do much better now and figure out what I want to be when I grow up. I am fabulous, healed, whole and healthy.

All those tools I learned in the treatment center are helping me now. If you have a problem, you need help. Please go for treatment. Stay in there. Do the work. Curse them out if you must. Go through the steps. I see now how all of it has helped me start living a healthier life. Many of the things we were taught in the treatment program remind me of my counseling sessions. It took me years to see the benefit.

I was asked once by a friend, "What was I missing?" I didn't know. I couldn't respond at first. "I didn't feel loved," I responded. I didn't realize I wasn't loving myself. I thought I was wonderful, so full of myself I couldn't even *see* myself. I tried so hard to make the world love me. I couldn't stand it if someone didn't love me. Again she asked, "What was I missing?"

Then I remembered. My purpose. I knew it at eight years old.

"God wants me to accomplish what He made me to do," I told my dad way back then. "Dad, how will I know?"

"You are already living it. You are perfect. Listen to your heart." He asked me, "Do you like the person you are?"

"I think I am great!" I answered.

"Will you always take care of yourself? Promise me," he said. I never kept that promise.

There is no shame
in beginning again,
for you get a chance
to build bigger
and better than before.

- recoveryexperts.com

"Angel Love" © Gloria Coppola

6

My Treasures

Have you ever gone on a treasure hunt? Picture this. Two crazy, free spirited gals, fellow pirates about to have a jolly ole time finding treasure. With limited time to gather up the 'goods' as they say, off we went. A little comical and adventurous, the two of us had a little fear, though nothing we couldn't handle together. By now, you know I can usually get in trouble. Or does trouble find me?

I told my divorce attorney there was something in the house I would like to have. He said to me, since I was still technically married, I had the right to get what I wanted. As always, I prayed to my son to give me a sign on what to do, as I questioned if this was the right way to proceed. In my prayers I could hear him say, "Go Mom! You've given up enough in life. Something really important is there for you. Don't be worried, I will protect you." I trusted his guidance. Away we went to the house, like two bandits.

When we pulled up to the estate, I tried the gate code a couple of times. Nothing happened. I almost turned the car around to leave when something inside of me said "Try the old code." Guess what? The gates started to open! Yep, the old code had Michael's favorite numbers in it. My assistant said "It's all going to be good. Michael has our back."

On to the hunt we went, a bit shaky because I didn't want any confrontations. We went in quickly to gather my belongings. Tip toeing into my dressing room as fast as we could, I noticed my jewelry box was gone. My heart sank and disappointment ran through me for a moment. Suddenly I noticed the real treasure was being revealed to me.

Oh my God! Michael's bubble gum machine! His bubblegum machine and lamp he made for me was right there! He loved them so much. What a true treasure! I was ecstatic. It was all I needed. "Let's get out of here," I said.

We didn't have quite the dangerous adventure we thought, but we certainly did have a ball. We came home like two pirate girls who found the booty. I had the most important thing money couldn't buy. It was all I needed. I was certainly learning about the real treasures in life these days.

The day I purchased my own home, I knew and trusted God would bring me the exact one meant for me. I was introduced to a woman who was a realtor. Her phone number had the same digits my son always loved, 4444. I fell in love with the house and was ready to begin a new life.

The first night I found myself standing out by the pool, looking at the colors changing and swirling in the water, the moonlight shining, and the soft lights around the lanai sparkling across the pool water.

I stood there, thanking God for everything in my life and mostly for my son. I was believing more in God than ever and He did take care of me. This is my Garden of Eden. I'm still living in a fairy tale in many ways, and I was off the pain meds for four years. It was the first time in my life I was making good decisions and I loved it.

God was about to give me another gift, a treasure I still hold dear in my heart. I always desired a little girl. After my hysterectomy, I thought that would be impossible.

Have you ever met someone, a stranger, and felt like you've known them your whole life? That's how I felt when I met Nissa. Her long, beautiful brown hair went down to her waist. She had huge brown eyes and an attitude to match it.

For her protection, Nissa had to leave her country of origin because of an onset of riots. She had been away from her mother for a while. I can't imagine how she was feeling. What a horrible feeling for a child. I just wanted to take her home with me and care for her.

On her first Christmas, we got to spend some time together. I really enjoyed watching her. She told me on this day, during one of our chats, she had noticed a stuffed animal on my bed. "Why would an adult have something like that?" she asked.

"Oh, that is Homer and he is an angel dog," I told her.

"He is?"

"He certainly is," I said. "He belonged to my son when he was alive. No matter how big he got, he loved his stuffed animals. This was his favorite one."

She listened attentively as I told her how I couldn't sleep, because I missed my son so much. Homer still smelled like Michael. Having the stuffed animal with me, I could feel like he was right there. I had slept with Homer for twenty six years. He goes everywhere with me.

"Wow he is special," she said. "I wish I had a Homer I could sleep with, because I'm very lonely here. I miss my mommy."

I couldn't sleep that night, thinking about Nissa and her loneliness. Should I check to see if I could care for her and take this little girl home with me. I could give her so many things, besides love and security. What am I thinking? Am I crazy? I'm fifty eight years old. I don't need an eight-year-old child to raise. The next morning, Nissa joined me while I was having my coffee. She started crying telling me she was going to miss me when I left

My heart melted. I went in my room, got Homer, and gifted it to her. I said, "Nissa would you like to have Homer keep you company while you're here?" "You would give me your special dog," she said, "when you don't even know me?"

"I know you're an Angel," I said. "Nissa, Homer has a magical power. He can talk to me no matter where he is, even if he's in a different country. He will let me know if you are lonely, scared or sad. He will let me know so I will always be connected to you. If you're ever missing me, talk to Homer, and he'll get the message to me."

Walking away without the dog, believe it or not, was one of the hardest things for me to do after twenty-six years. I gave a little girl some magic, comfort and security from an Angel. It was worth giving up my little friend for my new friend.

Days went by and I could not get that little beauty out of my head. I would swim and think how much Nissa would love the pool. I wondered how often she cried herself to sleep, scared and missing her mom. I sure remember having those moments in my life. I was hoping and praying Homer was taking good care of her with his magic.

The next day, I decided to pack up my car up and visit Nissa again. I wanted to surprise her. "Oh my God! I can't believe you are here!" she exclaimed with her little accent. "I was telling Homer how much I really missed you and love you. I prayed to him to bring you back to me. Homer really is magic!"

She ran over to embrace me and wrapped her arms around my legs. I spoke with her caretakers to see if they would be open to allowing me to take Nissa for a visit at my home. We all agreed it would be good for her and off we went to start a new adventure. This little treasure brought such joy into my life. I felt like I had a purpose again.

Her face was so cute when she walked into the house. She said, "Wow! This looks like the house in the movies." When she saw the pool, she immediately begged to get in it. "It's cold," I told her. "Give me a moment, I will turn the heater on for you."

"In my country," she said, "our water is ice and I'm a mermaid. So, it doesn't matter."

"Okay then, little miss mermaid." I watched her swim and laugh for hours. She made extra sure I would see every acrobatic mermaid move. She wanted to impress me, and I fell in love with her.

Nissa found Michael's Lego's in the closet one day. Actually, I had no idea they were there. We sat down and decided to build something. We said a pray together. She thanked Michael for the Lego's and we created lots of fun things. I decided to take her to Lego Land, an amusement park. She was so fun to watch. She even got an 'official' driver license and began bouncing around like the ball in a pin ball machine. Everything was new to her. Even though she had quite the bossy personality, she listened to my guidance.

When it was time to take her home, I just couldn't do it. I knew she was supposed to be with me longer. I called the caretakers, and all decided it would be a good thing for Nissa to continue to live with me for a while longer.

I became Nissa's American mommy. She loved the pool so much, I thought she was going to turn into a prune. I was exhausted trying to keep up with an eight-year-old, but I had never been happier. Nissa was not only a cute little girl, she was talented. When she expressed the desire to ride a horse, I couldn't wait to help her do it. I wanted her to have all the opportunities in America she could possibly have. She began taking horseback riding lessons a few months after she got here. The little stinker was winning horse shows after only a few months of lessons. I was home schooling, driving her to riding lessons, brushing the tangles out of her long hair. She screamed bloody murder in the mornings, fighting with me when it was time to get up. I never raised a little girl before and didn't realize how dramatic they are at times. It was very trying. I have to laugh because I'm quite sassy and dramatic too. A perfect match.

When that little Angel snuggled with me at night and laid her tiny head on my chest to thank me for loving her, my heart would melt even more. She said to me one night, "God is so good. I was scared when I came to America, but God took good care of me. He gave me another mommy, just like my mommy, to love me."

One of the best conversations, which will always remain with me, is how this wise little one knew so much. "Mommy," she said, "you had a lot of marriages. You need to know you should not let these men charm you like they do. They come to you like they're all that and a bowl of Wheaties." I nearly fell over with her analogy. "You fall for it, thinking they're wonderful. Then find out later they're not so nice, so you leave them. Why do you let these men charm you?" she asked. "You should have a man who will take good care of you and stay with you forever. You deserve it. You're wonderful and you're my Angel mommy." I had to hold back the laughter at first, then the tears as I took in her great wisdom. She was right.

From the mouths of babes. Yes, Nissa was smart, and she was a treasure to me. She went back home exactly one year later, on Christmas Eve, to live with her biological mother. I wouldn't trade my year with her for the world. I also have a great relationship with her mother over the Internet. She has thanked me so many times for taking care of her baby girl. I'm the one who should thank her, because if she were my little girl, I would want someone to take care of her. I will always be here for Nissa and her mom, whenever she needs me.

I have to say, though, as much as I knew she wanted her mom, it was hard to let her go. I got very depressed after she left. I convinced myself I was just exhausted from raising a little girl. Deep inside I was so sad. I couldn't get her out of my mind. Suddenly, my house felt lonely and quiet. It didn't seem so wonderful anymore.

I was sleeping all day again. I had no purpose, no reason to get up. One night I decided to take a little dip in the pool. I got out of bed, slipped off my nightgown, and forgot to bring a towel. When I got out of the pool, I rushed into the house to dry off. My wet feet slipped on the tile. Bam! I fell backwards on the hard surface. No way! This can't be happening to me again!

It turned out I had broken my tailbone and hurt my back. I cringed when the doctors offered me pain medication. I wanted to refuse it. I was so depressed, tired and in so much pain, I didn't care about my addiction anymore. I was also starting to tell myself again, "It's okay. I'll just take it while I'm healing and then I won't take it anymore." I had a way of convincing myself I could do anything, and this was temporary.

Where have I heard that before? Addiction never goes away. The desire for the drug never goes away. As soon as it hit me, I wanted more. Who was I kidding? When you've been an addict, your brain does funny things. No matter how long you stay off the drugs, it will still bring you right back to a full-blown addiction. It's a vicious cycle to deal with and an even harder one to kick.

Before I knew it, I was running to the hospital again to get my drugs, driving my doctor and pharmacist crazy, begging them for more pills and early refills. Concerned, the pharmacist called my doctor and told him he was over medicating me. Didn't stop me. I'm a drug addict. I gave him some great big sob story and he gave me another prescription. That's how it works when the doctor's a drug dealer. He doesn't care. It's like they give in so they don't have to listen to us, unaware and unattached to what is happening to us emotionally.

For the next four years, I would waste my life and money trying to get more pain pills. Again, I was either high or sleeping for days, detoxing. I had to sell my beautiful house because I was running out of money. I couldn't work with this drug addiction. Who would hire me? I was not reliable.

Prior to sharing this story, I overdosed and thought for sure I would die. Once again, my son saved me. I knew it was time to stop this insanity once and for all, quit lying to myself and stop letting the demon inside, the addict, win again.

There's a strong woman inside me. I know her and I want her back. I decided I did not want to waste any more of my life. I had to end this cycle and stop the control this deadly poison had over me for decades. I was pissing off friends, real friends, who loved me. I could not lose them nor the support they provided.

One friend suggested I get back in counseling while I was writing my story. Thank God I did! By looking at my patterns, I began finding out what triggers my addiction. I'm working with my therapist on the things which happened to me in childhood. I feel so free. It's saving my life, so I can start a new life. I'm starting to understand myself. It is really helping me forgive myself, too. I have hope for my future, where before I couldn't see far. Just months prior, I would be laying on the couch not caring about anything or anyone, ignoring phone calls and even the knock on the door from my neighbor. I still struggle with a lot of back pain, and the desire to numb it when it gets unbearable. I have tools to help me deal with the pain: massages, yoga, and meditation. Mostly, I have prayer.

I made a huge change when I moved back to my hometown. At the same time, I wrote a short story for another book with collaborative authors. I became a #1 bestselling author overnight! My reflection in the mirror shows nothing but love, peace, and happiness in my future. I hope to spread my message of inspiration, as much as I possibly can. I look forward to seeing my son again one day. For now, I'm not in a hurry and it feels Badass good!

My treasure has always been Michael. He went back to his Father. Nissa was another treasure God gave me temporarily and she went back to her mother. How blessed I am to have these treasures to hold forever in my heart.

I was hiding my greatest treasure right here at home. I wasn't being my authentic self. I wasn't even concerned about my own treasure. Now, I see the value of myself is the greater bounty. I don't have to steal anyone's treasure.

Living is a treasure. Loving myself is the biggest treasure! The best treasure of all? Sobriety! No wait! The best treasure is the love for God I'm feeling right now.

When you feel lost,
pause and look closely
around you.

Somewhere, somehow,
an Angel will be waiting to guide.

Let an Angel into your life
and comfort will follow you
wherever you go.

7

Love Letter to Michael

My Angel boy,

I cleaned your room today. I found the letter I left for you the night of the party. It was still folded and unread lying on your desk. You never did get to read it.

I was thinking of the last wonderful day we spent together. How glad I am that you made me go shopping with you. We had so many conversations, but the one I remember hit me like a ton of bricks in my heart. "One day, Mom, you are going to wish I was here and wanting to spend time with me." It was that conversation that pulled me out of bed from my drug-induced stupor to be with you. I had no idea how true that statement was going to be. How I wish I could see your handsome face now. If I had to, I would give up the rest of my life for a chance to get one of those Big Bear hugs you used to give me every day.

I sat down after you left for the graduation party, to write you a 'proud mama' note. Michael, you have no idea how proud I had become. You probably know that by now, listening to me from heaven all these years bragging about you. Do ears ring in heaven?

As I wrote the note, I shared a few pearls of wisdom for your future. Little did I even conceive in that moment your future would be spent being my Angel in heaven instead of my Angel on earth.

It took on a whole new meaning for me. I read my own words, telling you how much I would miss you. Anytime I ever left you a note, you would just give me a big hug and say, "Thanks Mom, I think you are the best too." I neatly folded up the letter to place it back on your desk when I noticed an envelope sticking out of one of the drawers. It caught my attention, as if it were calling out to me. I could hear you saying, "Mom, those notes meant the world to me." I carefully opened the drawer wondering what I would uncover. There it was. A box containing all the letters I had ever written you over the years. I had no idea you saved them. An overwhelming feeling of emotions ran through my heart as I picked one up. It was a love letter from you to me, that I never did receive, until now.

"Dear Mom, these letters have been the only thing that have kept me going during rough times throughout the years. You were always the best mother in the world and always let me know I was the greatest kid that God ever made. I realize how blessed I am that He gave me to you." Letters like this are a mother's dream, not a nightmare.

You gave me hope and love today by writing that letter to me, son. My consolation was knowing that you're still here to watch over me. Your undying love for me has brought me comfort many times. There are always reminders you send me at the perfect time, baby boy. It is always a comfort knowing you are still here, and you haven't left my side.

Michael, when I hear Elvis's song *The Wonder of You* I always think of you. "When no one else can understand me, when everything I do is wrong, you give me love and consolation, you give me hope to carry on." That's you, my son.

No truer words could express my feelings. "Your love to me is worth a fortune. Your love for me is everything. I guess I'll never know the reasons why you love me like you do." That's the wonder of you, Michael. I know you always loved this song and now it is mine to you.

Standing here with this letter in my hand, I wondered why you didn't give it to me? Did you leave it knowing I would need it today to help me get through this horrible, dreadful task ahead of me? Perhaps. Did you have a feeling you were going to die?

Remember when you were four years old? You needed to learn how to become organized. You got so upset when you couldn't find your favorite toy. Mom put up shelves on your walls. I drew pictures of each toy on the wall. It helped you see where everything belonged easily. Such a little thing we did together made you so happy.

I couldn't open the door to your room today. I was frozen. It had been closed for six months. The mere thought of it, smelling you, knowing I would never be able to see you again, was too much to handle. The first thing I noticed when I opened the door was your t-shirt and socks on the floor, the ones you wore earlier that day. You had tossed them there, as you typically did. I never touched them in all this time. I picked them up, held them to my face and prayed, "Please God, let me smell him." Just maybe his scent might be there after all these months. I imagined in my mind I could smell the Drakkar cologne you loved to wear but to my disappointment Michael, it didn't smell like you anymore. How will I go on when this is all gone and I take your room apart? It will all disappear forever. How could I walk in here never seeing your bed, your clothes again? Tears flowed down my cheeks, my nose stuffed up from crying, as I picked up your clothes for the last time. No mother should have to go through this, ever! No longer can I complain how stinky your feet were. Boy, I would give just about anything right now to smell them. I have to giggle, Michael. "Did God let you get close to him smelling like that?"

We surely made some great memories in our short lifetime together. I can still hear you say, "Mom I love my room, let's organize all my magazines on that new rack." I'm looking at them now. Those magazines were very special to you. They were kept in perfect condition. You told me, "One day they'll be worth a fortune."

Michael, you were such a tender heart, always looking for the good. You loved your dad so much even though he didn't live with us. I'm sorry for that, son. I wish you had met him earlier in your life. I know he loved you dearly and the bond was instant when you first met at twelve. You had all the good from him in you, just like a carbon copy. Your wisdom was beyond your years. You told me how much it meant to you that we were able to raise you together in separate homes and still be friends.

Son, I'm getting so dizzy from the tears in my eyes. They are blinding me. It's so exhausting. How will I ever get rid of anything of yours? I took a moment to sit on your bed, quiet my mind and relax into my heart. There above your bed was a shelf. Immediately I saw the sparkling silver band you always wore every day of your life. Why didn't you wear it that night to the party? Did you leave it for me to find? When I wrapped it on my garter on my wedding day, I felt you walked me down that aisle.

I can still see your angel head laying on your pillow. Resting tenderly each night on this bed, you would drift off to your dream world. One night I was so busy doing laundry and catching up on chores, I didn't say good night. You ran down to me and said, "Mom, I can't go to sleep without you tucking me in, praying with me and kissing me good night." Oh, to have those precious moments we often take for granted. I'm so choked up right now, I must pray. I will kneel beside your bed and ask God.

I pray now; who am I gonna give this bed to? What am I gonna do with all these things? What am I gonna keep and what am I gonna give away? It's tough going through your personal items especially since I always tried to give you privacy. I never realized how difficult it is for someone who loses a loved one. Once you get rid of everything, the reality sets in. They are gone.

Just then, the phone rang. It was your favorite friend, Aunt Pam, asking me if I knew anyone who could repair a bed. Hers had broken. It was old and worn out. She said she was even embarrassed for someone to see the mattress. I had a great idea. I suggested she take your bed! How thrilled she was and I got to help someone because of you. We were both so happy.

Then it hit me when I got home and saw that empty space where the bed used to be. Barren.

My heart was being ripped apart, like daggers slicing through it. It felt exactly like the day I saw you lying in the casket. I had to face the truth you were gone permanently. I fell to my knees outside your room, cried like a baby and prayed to God for help. I wished you would just walk through the door and make this pain go away. The loss was unbearable. I would never have another room for you in my home. Too many changes were happening quickly, and I was going over the edge. I had tremendous fear wondering how to live my life without you. I wanted to die now, so I could be with you. What if I just take all those pills and end this finally. I could get to heaven and be with you for eternity.

On the way to my room, I had a plan to take enough pills that would ensure my death. I noticed a mysterious cassette tape and a magazine laying on my bed. It was from your favorite teacher. You know, the one who talked you into doing that speech about diversity your senior year.

Did an angel put this here? It doesn't really matter, does it? Angels are always around me. I played the cassette and heard your voice. Oh My God! You were speaking to me. "Don't fight changes in your life. Embrace them, celebrate them." Michael, you saved my life in that moment. I had to make a different choice. Dying was not the answer. I heard from your own voice, "Don't fight the changes in your life, Mom." Wow, a quick shift in my perspective and I was going to celebrate by making your favorite food; fried green tomatoes.

I can't thank you enough for always being my angel. I can't count the times you have been there for me. I know I made many mistakes. I feel you forgave me. I know I did my best. "God's plan, Mom. He always sends the angels when we need them." I can still hear those words echo in my head.

Michael, even as I cry in this moment, I have challenging days. I promise, though, you won't have to cry anymore watching me try to kill myself. Even after your death, you always provided me the right message at the perfect time. I know it's you. Thirty years of craziness, of not living a life I could love and be happy. I had everything and lost it. I had great strength to overcome all the adversities. Surely, I can find my happiness. I promise Michael, I plan on celebrating life. I have missed so much.

I will honor your life. I will learn to honor mine and honor God. I feel appreciative to God instead of just muttering the words. I truly feel it now.

I am so proud of myself right now. In this moment nothing is numbing me out. I feel everything more than I could ever imagined. I know I loved deeply because I feel deeply.

Reflections now become self-reflection as I take ownership of loving myself.

I always said I was going to write the "Greatest American Love Story" and here it is. Michael you are my greatest love. This is our story.

Love from my heart to yours,

Mom

The more you believe in Angels,
the more you see them all around,
in friends, family and acquaintances.

It's amazing how much
goodness you can see
if only you believe.

Wherever you go,
whatever you do,
may God's Angels
watch over you.

Conclusion

If I could go back and do things over, I would think about the decisions I had made. If one of my parents would have mentioned education or college, I believe my life would have been different because I did have dreams. I didn't know there were options and choices in my life beyond getting married and having kids. Now I understand more about why I made these decisions. My upbringing influenced me tremendously, with all the observations implanted without my knowing and or even realizing it. I know I can do more, be more, be different and healthier. Gosh, I wish I didn't wait so long. God has given me this opportunity and I am taking it.

If someone had suggested more counseling after I was raped, I would have made better decisions with men. I was only eleven, how could I know. If I knew how to look at people differently, evaluate their character, I would have had a different life. I was too trusting.

If I was more educated, I could have supported myself better. I would have been a marine biologist. That was my dream! I wanted to work with dolphins or whales. I was twenty three when I got my GED and wanted to be a doctor. I didn't have the support to succeed, so it never came to fruition. Dad called a GED the "Good Enough Diploma." I loved that!

My message to those who are struggling out there, "Make a choice. Stay sick or get well. Get help and reach out. Be honest with people."

I can personally say when I quit and fell off the wagon, it was a choice. We make them even if we don't know the difference. Always decide which way you want to be. I finally got sick and tired of being sick and tired. Which life did I really want? I had to really be honest and make a decision for myself. I was always trying for someone else, my parents, husbands, etc. I didn't have the desire bad enough for myself, until now.

I am so happy and excited to live now.

I don't need anything when I get to heaven. I'll have all I need with me. I will be bringing a ton of good memories and love in my heart with me when I check in. I'll be holding my angel son and I will be kissing God and thanking him for all the blessings he has given me in life.

I know God expects us to do these kind things. It sure feels good to me and that's why I do it. That's my reward.

"Praise the Lord,
you his Angels,
you Mighty Ones
who do his bidding,
who obey his word."

psalms 103:20

Epilogue

Does God make some people stronger than others? Is a child of God made stronger by the trials and tribulations He has given us in life? Or does God put the tougher things on the ones He made stronger?

I can answer this from my personal opinion and experiences in life. I am absolutely no stronger than anyone else and am actually weaker in a lot of ways than most. We are all made the same. We are all made through God's perfect design and sent to Earth to carry out His plans.

I believe those that He knows will make a difference from their experiences by sharing them and sharing the lessons they have learned, He gives just a little more to carry in life.

God has given me so many blessed experiences in life. Some very hard lessons I've learned. I've had to grab myself and pull myself up again from the depths of depression and disappointments and change my whole life many times.

We don't get to choose what happens to us so many times in life, but we always have the choice in how we deal with it, where our attitude sits, and what good we're going to try to bring out of every bad situation.

Believe me my friends, happiness is a choice. Happiness is not a place you find yourself in, or that some lover or partner brings to you. Happiness is a choice we make.

When my son Michael died thirty years ago, I knew that my life was not going to end and I had two choices. I could either get through it with a great attitude and continue my loving relationship with God and thank Him for that child He gave me in the first place, or I could have gotten bitter and angry and made everyone around me suffer along with me.

I choose to take my son's life and celebrate it everyday. Instead of being sad that he is no longer on this Earth with me, I am happy that I had him in the first place for eighteen years. God gave me an Angel and I choose to honor God, and my son's life, by continually trying to keep my attitude good, my spirit bright, and try to help someone else just a little bit to find their smile again.

For those of you who do not know, I had a traumatic fall from a third floor balcony in 1978 and for over thirty years, I have suffered with chronic pain. Still today, I am in pain in my back and legs 24/7, but I do my best just try to spread a little bit of love in this world.

My son left this earth with no more than $20 in his pocket. He was the richest boy on earth and so loved.

One thing I "learned" when my son left this world is love is the only thing you take with you. It's important to contribute to this world and improve your friend's lives along with your loved ones. Today, 30 years later his step brother and friends are still writing stories about him and missing him dearly. That, my friends, is success.

I am glad to be a successful woman. I choose to be that way and everyday of my life I continuously choose to try to do a little better and bring a little joy to everyone around me. I love you all so much and I appreciate you letting me vent all of my thoughts and stories with you here.

You can be happy starting today, just make that choice. Do you want to be happy or sad? It really is that simple. You just have to practice a lot.

I am a warrior of God. I'm seeking to be a stronger, more peaceful and happy woman. My struggles are hard, they're real and some days I can barely get through the day. Yet I still choose happiness, help and prayer, which I practice daily. God bless you all.

~ A-Dora-ble

Dora Sherry

is a Champion Badass Survivor
in life's challenges. This
multiple time cancer survivor
has been shot, stabbed, and
lived two years in a wheelchair
after being thrown from a third-
floor balcony not knowing if
she would ever walk again.
There have been many more
experiences like this in her life,
but without a doubt, the two
biggest challenges she has had to survive are the death
of her only child at 18 in 1990 and an opiate addiction
that has held her prisoner for 40 years .

Badass Dora got up and out of that wheelchair after two
years. She became a third-degree black belt in Kenpo
karate. That's how she's gone through everything,
especially her son's death; like a champion. Champions
don't look back. They concentrate on now and
forward. Sometimes they are so strong though, that they
forget to take care of that heart and hurt inside of them.

*This is my story. I have had angels around me through
all my life. I thank them for rescuing me from some
extremely dangerous situations many times. I thank
God for sending those angels to me. I am thankful that
I recognize them in every form. I love God for all the
challenges I've had in life. They have made me the
woman I am today. With all my heart, "If I weren't me,
I would wish I were."*

Custom Designed Cover
and Book Interior

1:1 Personal Writing Coaching
and Author Support through
the entire process

Journals & Planners
We create these too.

love yourself

Marketing
Assistance

including
Amazon
Key word
and
Category
search

Your Amazing
Custom designed
cover here!

Solo Authors
Up to 60,000
words

Collaborative
Authors
3,500 words

including
full editing for
everyone!

ORACLE CARD DECKS
Yes, we create these too!

YOUR STORY HERE!

www.PPP-Publishing.com
828-713-3521
gloria@gloriacoppola.com

Powerful
Potential and Purpose

PUBLISHING

Made in the USA
Middletown, DE
06 July 2020